The American Assembly, *Columbia University*

STATE LEGISLATURES
IN AMERICAN POLITICS

Prentice-Hall, Inc., *Englewood Cliffs, N.J.*

Preface

Edited by Alexander Heard, Chancellor of Vanderbilt U
comprised the background reading for the Twenty-ninth
on State Legislatures, April 28-May 1, 1966, at Arden
American Assembly on the Harriman (N.Y.) campus of
It is also intended for regional Assemblies on this sub
university use, and for general readership.

The opinions found herein are those of the authors. As
tional institution The American Assembly takes no officia
National Municipal League to be associated with individu
a citizens organization for better government, supported t
as part of a five-year project for the improvement of state

Cli
Pre
Th

Table of Contents

Alexander Heard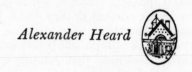

Introduction—Old Problem, New Context

The behavior of American state legislatures has disquieted the informed public for over a century. Since World War II, frauds and inadequacies in particular states have been exposed by popular magazine articles and by professional studies, and the changing position of state legislatures generally in the American federal system has frequently been the subject of comment, and often of lament. In 1965 a spate of efforts were put in motion by educators, foundations, civic organizations, and legislators themselves to improve the performance and increase the significance of these much mocked political institutions.

Showmanship has not been lacking among the people's legislative representatives. It would be easy to get the idea that bib overalls, raucous jokes, country ballads, ready fists, and an eccentric sense of priority in debating the public business characterize all state legislators all the time. They do not, of course, but beyond the bizarre episodes that reporters relish, deadly serious charges of corruption are leveled at many legislators. The charges often emanate from impeccable sources and are supported by credible evidence.

They range from allegations of personal bribery to the doleful conclusion that much of the time these institutions of representative government so conduct themselves that the popular will is thwarted. Even if all legislators were models of efficiency and rectitude, as indeed some of them are, most state legislatures would remain poorly organized and technically ill equipped to do what is expected of them. They do not meet

ALEXANDER HEARD *is Professor of Political Science and Chancellor, Vanderbilt University. He was Chairman of the President's Commission on Campaign Costs (1961-62), and is a former President of the Southern Political Science Association, former Vice President of the American Political Science Association, and at one time participated in local political activities. Chancellor Heard's writings include* A Two-Party South? *and* The Costs of Democracy.

often enough nor long enough; they lack space, clerical staffing, professional assistance; they are poorly paid and overworked; they are prey to special interests, sometimes their own; their procedures and committee systems are outmoded; they devote inordinate time to local interests that distract them from general public policy; they sometimes cannot even get copies of bills on which they must vote. They work, in short, under a host of conditions that dampen their incentive and limit their ability to function effectively.

In nations all around the world, the effectiveness and viability of legislative bodies have been of concern in the twentieth century. In the United States, various measures of renovation are regularly proposed for the national Congress. American state legislatures have been objects of attention, too. The racy episodes, testimonies of chicanery, examples of institutional inefficiency, and citations of declining function that stud the discourse yield to a layman the impression that state legislatures are an archaic jungle of mysterious machinations, and that something ought to be done about it.

Reform of American governmental institutions is normally preceded by decades of discussion, with advances made in fits and starts when made at all. So it was with the state legislatures—until 1962. The background papers for the 1955 American Assembly on "The Forty-Eight States" cited the misrepresentativeness of state legislatures as urgently requiring remedy, and gave the faulty legislative apportionments then prevailing as a principal block to public confidence in state government itself. *Baker v. Carr*, in 1962, began a series of court decisions that upset long-entrenched patterns of representation and led down the road to apportionment in all state legislatures on the principle of "one man, one vote." This radical development solved what was thought to be the number one problem, a problem annually becoming more acute as the nation's population grew and became more mobile. It came at a time when more balanced competition between political parties in state politics had begun to appear. In some areas, where previously one party had dominated the legislative chambers, the way was being opened through strengthened party competition to a more effective organization of legislative political power.

With these developments came a change in outlook toward the whole future of state legislatures. Now, perhaps, other changes could be made, changes in their structure and functioning to enable them to play better their proper role, or even a more significant role, in the American political system.

This volume sets forth the context in which state legislatures operate and in which proposals for altering their behavior must be evaluated. The authors have not been asked to chart a road to salvation. They analyze the characteristics and behavior of existing state legislatures and identify the forces that must be understood in assessing legislative performance and in seeking to change it. State legislatures make many important decisions. They enact bills into law. They may oversee the activities of state agencies. As representative assemblies they perform important symbolic functions. In these and other tasks state legislative performance is shaped and limited by powerful forces.

The increased significance of government generally in American life means that state legislatures are part of an increasingly pervasive system of political decision making. At the same time, the center of gravity in this system has shifted steadily to the federal level. Within the state's own processes, the legislature's constitutional areas of discretion have often been contracted, for example, by federal matching requirements that automatically commit large sums that might otherwise be spent in the legislature's discretion for different purposes, and earmarking of state revenues, by the legislature itself, for specified purposes. Such leadership as the state legislature may have is frequently found outside its own membership, often in a governor. And the ability of a legislature to act in politically effective ways may be determined by the structure of factional and partisan political power in the state outside the legislature as well as inside it. The state legislature, in other words, is part of a highly complex and variously integrated federal political system whose many elements impinge on what state legislatures should and can do.

The nation itself changes constantly, often in profound ways that affect the functions government undertakes and the expectations held in different quarters of how state legislatures should behave. The volume of needed legislation, its technical character, the cost of implementing much of it, and many other pressures that bear on state legislatures in particular, and on American government generally, originate outside the control of legislators, indeed often beyond the significant influence of any political personnel.

Some variations among the fifty states are deep and lasting. They give unique qualities to the social and economic setting in which state government operates, to the kinds of people who become legislators, and to the kinds of problems these legislators try to solve. Despite certain common characteristics, each of the fifty state legislatures, indeed each of their 99 legislative houses, has a life of its own. Individuality in custom more than in constitution sets each body off from the others.

State legislatures may be our most extreme example of institutional lag. In their formal qualities they are largely nineteenth century organizations and they must, or should, address themselves to twentieth century problems. Can they now perform, or be made capable of performing in the future, the great functions of representation, reconciliation, and legitimization that are required of legislatures in our time? Is the institutional lag that has characterized state legislatures symptomatic of all government in the United States?

However one answers these questions, eventually he must also ask himself what action is possible. What can be altered, made better? What are the points of leverage where pressure can be exerted to bring about improvement?

The National Municipal League, the Council of State Governments, other organizations, and many individuals have advocated concrete changes in the ways our state legislatures are chosen, are organized, and do their business. For three-quarters of a century improvements have been made progressively in equipping state legislatures to do their business. The states have varied widely among themselves in the innovations they have adopted. The achievements of certain states demonstrate clearly that other states can do significantly more than they have done so far to prepare their legislatures to perform well. But there are fundamental boundaries, too, even after *Baker v. Carr,* that confine legislatures in what they do and how they do it. Much of our task is to understand what can usefully be done to improve the performance of these historic political bodies. Toward this understanding the following papers are addressed.

Herbert Jacob

1

Dimensions of State Politics

Once every year or two, life becomes more exciting at state capitals. Often located in small, out-of-the-way towns, they are scarcely distinguishable from other small cities except for this change of pace that occurs whenever the state legislature convenes. This event brings with it an influx of lobbyists, the arrival of reporters, and numbers of politically interested citizens. The state government of course continues to operate when the legislature is recessed, but its tasks are usually so routine that its operations proceed with little public notice. In some states, even governors, the most newsworthy of state officials, have been known to travel to the state's major city to call a press conference to get better coverage.

The excitement generated by the convening of the legislature may mislead us in assessing its importance, but it represents well the legislature's central symbolic role in state politics. Its functions are important to citizens as well as to government officials.

Functions of State Legislatures

Every schoolboy has learned that legislators represent the people. History has known many an autocratic executive, but legislatures have rarely been the engine of oppression. In America, they function as a check on the executive; they are also instrumental in integrating public demands with public policy. As we shall see in later chapters, the performance of this function is no easy task because the people rarely know what they want and in so far as they do know, they are often divided

HERBERT JACOB *is Associate Professor of Political Science at the University of Wisconsin. He has contributed articles to numerous journals and has authored* Studies in Judicial Politics *(with Kenneth N. Vines) and* Justice in America, *among others. Professor Jacob was also the editor (with Kenneth N. Vines) of* Politics in the American States.

among themselves. Nevertheless, regardless of whether a particular legislature does well or badly its job of representing, the fact that it is dedicated to this function gives it importance, because representation is central to the American democratic ideal. The legislature is symbolic of this belief. Legislators frequently speak in the vocabulary of "representation" and justify their decisions in terms of what they think the people want or should have.

Quite apart from this symbolic significance of legislatures, they are also significant because their decisions affect many people. State legislatures consider thousands of proposals each year, and pass many of them into law. Most concern only a few citizens, but some are as significant as many of the laws enacted by the United States Congress. Each time the legislature meets it may alter the taxes which its citizens pay to the state. It decides the manner in which the state's funds are to be spent, thus affecting levels of health, education, welfare, and other services which the state's people may enjoy. The legislature must approve all new programs in which the state government participates, including many originated by the federal government. It also decides which old programs are to be abandoned or shifted to another level of government. It sets many of the policies that regulate the business and financial affairs of numerous enterprises in the state, and the professional and occupational careers of large numbers of its citizens.

A third function that state legislatures sometimes perform explicitly, but in which they are always involved implicitly, is the supervision of the state's administrative agencies. Legislatures control the purse strings of the state and use their power of appropriation to influence administrative performance.

The Legislature's Position in State Political Systems

Although legislatures perform important functions in every state, they do their work differently and frequently come to different results in each state. To understand these variations we need to consider the political setting as well as the social and economic environments in which legislatures operate. It is particularly important that we recognize the systemic position of legislatures so that we may avoid the pre-Copernican fallacy of presuming that what we are most interested in is the center of the universe.

The concept of political systems has recently been carefully described by David Easton in his book, *A Systems Analysis of Political Life*. Adapting his model for our needs, we may conceive of the universe in which state legislatures operate as consisting of the following elements: their physical, social, and cultural environment; the people who perceive this environment in such a way that they are led to give or withhold support for their state government and/or make demands of it; the channels

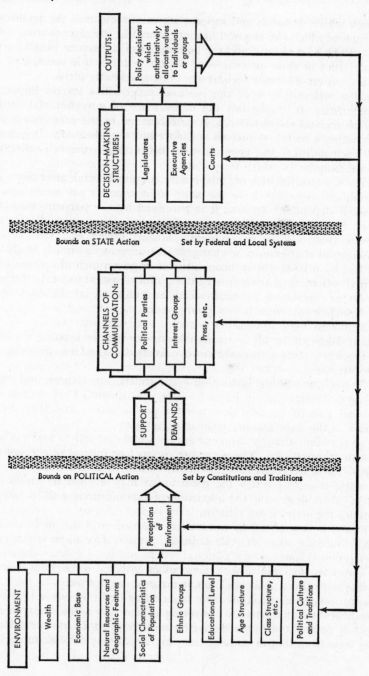

through which demands and support are communicated; the agencies of government which can respond to those demands; the repercussions (feedback) of official decisions; and the boundaries of the system which restrict the activities of state governments. Figure 1 shows this concept of the political universe of state legislatures in diagrammatic form.

Such a systemic view of the political process has several important characteristics. It emphasizes the dependence of governmental institutions on societal characteristics. It reveals many of the intervening variables between social conditions and governmental decisions. It helps us place each political and governmental institution in the full context of the environment in which it operates.

Certain characteristics of this model require special attention. The environment does not have the same impact under all conditions. Its impact is dependent on how it is perceived by the participants in the system. Some people will view poverty, for instance, with dismay and generate demands for governmental action; others will view it as a phenomenon that cannot be changed; still others will view it as changeable but by private philanthropy instead of governmental action. Thus, the perceptions of participants in the political system are extremely important in translating physical, social, and cultural conditions into demands on the government or support for it.

The means used to channel demands and supports may also be important. Some are highly institutionalized, like the press, political parties, and interest groups. Others are more individualized, such as petitions and demonstrations.

The decision-making institutions—the courts, legislatures, and executive agencies—take many forms in state government. They do not play an equal role in meeting demands for public action and they do not operate in the same manner from state to state.

The decisions that government agencies make or fail to make is what interests most citizens. These are the product or output of the political system. These decisions also take many forms: some are concerned with collecting resources which the government may use for its public programs; others determine the allocation of expenditures; a third category regulates the activities of citizens.

Finally, it is essential to understand the various kinds of boundaries which limit the scope of state political systems. The states coexist with other political systems—the national system and local systems. Sometimes the states are in conflict with these other systems; often they must cooperate with them. Another limit is imposed on the states by their own constitutions which prohibit them from engaging in certain activities.

Each of these characteristics of state political systems impinges in some direct or indirect way on state legislatures. Each state's system differs in some ways from that of its neighbors, making it very difficult to speak in

general terms about American state politics. In their general characteristics, however, state political systems closely resemble each other because
social conditions, political and governmental institutions, and public programs are similar, even if not identical, throughout the United States. To
discern the similarities and differences and assess the importance of each
element of the political system will be the main task of this chapter.

What the States Do

Let us begin with the outputs of state political systems. State
governments are distinguished from the national and local governments
largely by what they do and do not do. Unlike the national government,
states are only slightly involved, when involved at all, in expenditures for
defense, foreign relations, or space exploration, functions that consume
more than half the national budget. Instead, they are wholly dedicated
to internal affairs. Unlike local governments, the states often do not staff
the operating agencies which actually carry out programs. With many
programs, state governments set policy and supervise the administration
conducted by local units of government.

We may classify the output of political systems into three categories.
State systems are heavily involved in each of them.

First, political systems make decisions to collect resources for common
use, generally through taxation measures. The states are themselves heavy
taxers and they supervise the additional taxes imposed by local governments. Together, state and local political systems collect about half as
much tax revenue as the national government does.

The second output of political systems consists of decisions to allocate
the government's resources, to spend the taxes which it has collected.
Since a government may possess resources in addition to those which it
has taxed (receipts from commercial enterprises, from license fees and
service charges, and from intergovernmental grants, its expenditure decisions are not simply the obverse side of its taxation decisions.

Finally, political systems may regulate the activities of their subjects
and citizens. The government may restrict, regulate, or protect citizens in
the exercise of their civil liberties; it may regulate or protect economic
activities, including many professions; and it polices the lives of its
citizens, protecting them from those who would exploit them if left to
their own devices.

Although each of the fifty states performs functions in all three categories, no two states have identical patterns of taxation, expenditures,
or regulation. State legislatures, and other decision-making branches of
government, have sometimes responded differently to the same stimuli.
We need to understand these variations if we are to assess the role of state
legislatures accurately.

TAXATION PATTERNS

By every available measure, the states differ greatly among themselves in the amount of taxes they raise and the manner in which they do so. In order to measure the amount of taxation accurately it is necessary to include local taxation as well, since some states divert large sums of their own revenues to the localities, precluding heavy local tax rates, while other states keep most of their own revenues and force the localities to raise large sums by themselves. Throughout the country, state governments supervise and restrict local taxation. Using a joint measure of state and local taxation, we find that in recent years some states have raised twice the per capita amount that other states collected. Similar variations exist when we examine the amount of tax revenues collected per $1,000 personal income. The state that raised the lowest amount per $1,000 personal income, Virginia with $73.98 in 1962, collected barely more than 60 per cent the amount that Vermont collected that year, $117.81. Although individual states differ slightly from year to year in comparison with their neighbors, these variations have survived for many decades. There is every reason to expect that they will continue to do so.

The states also have made quite different decisions about how they collect their tax revenues. Although most Americans are familiar with both sales and income taxes, states have differed considerably in their reliance on them. In the early 1960s, as Clara Penniman has shown in *Politics in the American States,* only 14 states depended heavily on an income tax while 29 states leaned more on a sales tax. In addition, there were 7 states that used neither tax very much but relied instead on the property tax or on taxes levied on the oil and gas industries.

A decision about what tax to impose is one of the most crucial made by state legislatures and governors. As governors have learned, although it may be necessary to impose new taxes to meet popular demands for services, a decision to do so may well cost them re-election. Such decisions are difficult to make because they so immediately affect large portions of a state's population, and are visible to every voter. In dollars and cents, the difference that an income or sales tax makes to many voters, however, is slight. The choice of one or another tax has become controversial because of the value commitments attached to each tax. Businessmen favor and labor unions oppose the sales tax because, when it is imposed on most retail purchases, it is relatively regressive. Income taxes attract precisely the opposite constellation of support and opposition since they may be relatively progressive if graduated. The outcome in most states is a series of compromises. Many states do not impose a general sales tax but use a selective tax which is not quite so regressive; even more of the income tax states do not have a sharply graduated tax. Consequently, differences in the regressiveness of state taxation are less than the debates about the taxes would lead us to believe.

In addition to the income and sales taxes, the states also rely on a wide variety of other fiscal measures. In every state the property tax is used; in most it is now principally reserved for local use but in some states, like Arizona, Nebraska, and Wyoming, it is still an important source of state revenues. Every state also levies taxes on motor fuels and generally uses these taxes to finance highway construction and maintenance. As a result of incentives provided by the national government's inheritance tax structure, each state also has an inheritance tax, although it provides over 5 per cent of the state's revenue only in Connecticut, New Hampshire, and New Jersey. Every state also levies taxes on alcoholic beverages and these taxes bring more money than the inheritance tax; in ten states they produce more than 5 per cent of the state's revenue, the high occurring in Vermont where liquor taxes brought in 8.9 per cent of Vermont's tax revenues in 1962. All but three states levy tobacco taxes; and because tobacco has more widespread usage than alcohol, it brings in slightly more revenue to the states. Finally, a few states have the opportunity to levy special taxes on industries that are peculiarly important within their borders. This is particularly true of oil-rich states like Louisiana, Oklahoma, and Texas which derive a considerable portion of their tax revenues from severance taxes on oil and natural gas producers.

As Clara Penniman has indicated, fundamental decisions about the imposition of a new kind of state tax occur rarely. Such decisions are the subject of long, bitter debate, but once made they are seldom repealed. After a state legislature has decided to impose a new tax, the state's revenues usually suffice for a number of years. Attention then shifts to the problem of how its funds shall be spent. While the legislature is in a dominant position to accept, reject, or alter recommendations to tax, it is in a weaker position in passing on decisions to spend.

EXPENDITURE PATTERNS

The states and their local governments control between 40 and 45 per cent of all government expenditures in the United States. Until the adoption of Medicare, federal aid to education, and the poverty program under the Johnson Administration, most of the growth in domestic expenditures was accounted for by state and local programs, not by the federal government. Even with the new federal programs for "The Great Society," state and local governments continue to bear the burden of services which require increasing expenditures.

The same kind of variation exists in expenditure patterns as in taxation patterns. The state with the lowest per capita general expenditures in 1962 (South Carolina with $201.70) spent less than half that of four other states (Alaska, California, Nevada, and Wyoming).

Throughout the country, the largest state expenditures are allocated to education, highways, welfare, and public health programs. Correction and police programs and general grants to local governments rank lower but nevertheless account for about 5 per cent of the total.

The way in which each state cuts its expenditure pie reflects local conditions, traditions, and preferences. New Mexico and Utah spend about half their state budget on education, mostly in aid to local public schools; this reflects their tradition of relatively weak local support for education. Massachusetts and New Hampshire force their local governments to bear most of the burden of public education and devote less than 20 per cent of their total expenditures to education. The same variation occurs with highway expenditures. Five states (Nebraska, New Hampshire, South Dakota, Vermont, and Wyoming) spend more than two-fifths of their state funds on highway construction and maintenance; at the other extreme, Hawaii spends less than 10 per cent of its funds on similar projects. Even welfare expenditures vary, despite the influence of the federal government's grant programs, because the states differ widely as to the degree of local financing required for general assistance. In Missouri, almost one-quarter of the state's expenditures go to welfare; Alaska, Georgia, Indiana, Virginia, and Wyoming, however, spend only 5 per cent or less.

Within each broad sphere of expenditures, the states also vary a great deal in what they emphasize and how they seek to accomplish their goals. Educational expenditures provide a good example. Every state provides some aid to local school districts, but their method of doing so is rarely the same. Some states make flat grants-in-aid—the same per pupil to each school district; some try to equalize school expenditures in rich and poor districts; some try to prod local spending by giving incentive grants to those districts that are trying hard to provide adequate educational funds. Some states put most of their money on general grants for local education; others put more into paricular programs they are trying to promote in their local schools. In each state these goals are expressed in extremely complicated grant formulas over which interest groups vie intensively and legislatures toil for many hours.

Moreover, although every state has a system of public higher education, the states differ enormously in the amount of support they give to their state colleges and universities. In states with strong traditions of private higher education, the public systems were starved until the tidal wave of college-bound students in the early 1960s forced a more adequate state response. Nevertheless, New York continues to export thousands of its students for lack of space in its own colleges and universities. Massachusetts and New York, two of our wealthiest states, spent less per capita on higher education than did Arkansas and Mississippi in 1962.

The states also differ greatly in the degree to which they subsidize their local governments. In 1962, for instance, New York and Wisconsin spent almost half of all their funds in payments to local governments. In New York, these payments consisted of more than $100 million in general aid to local governments, more than $850 million to support the state's public schools and local colleges, over $90 million for highway aid, almost $350 million for public welfare programs, almost $50 million for health programs, and an additional $50 million for miscellaneous programs. Only five states spent more for all their government functions than New York spent to aid its local governments. In contrast to the large expenditures by New York and Wisconsin, New Hampshire and South Dakota use less than 10 per cent of their funds for grants to local governments.

The decision by the state government to grant substantial aid to its local subdivisions is a crucial one. It shifts the burden of many local programs to the state government. It also provides an incentive for establishing a powerful local government lobby which operates in the state capitol to safeguard its subsidies. Although state subsidies justify state supervision of local programs, the states usually do not insist on close control because local governments resent what they consider to be encroachments on their autonomy. The consequence is that states find themselves footing the bill for programs over which they exercise slight supervision. The localities receiving state funds rarely are given a strong incentive to be frugal with such funds. Yet, seen from another perspective, extensive state-aid programs bring substantial benefits of two sorts. First, they permit the state to equalize the resources of its various areas and thus to promote a relatively similar standard of services even in locales that lack their own resources. Second, such state-aid programs shift the burden from local property owners to other tax payers. Since local governments usually can levy only the most regressive taxes, substantial state-aid programs tend to make the entire tax structure somewhat less regressive than might otherwise be the case.

STATE REGULATORY ACTIVITIES

Expenditures do not sufficiently measure all state government decisions. Many significant activities require relatively small expenditures. This is particularly true of the many regulatory programs that states sponsor.

Since the latter part of the nineteenth century, state governmens have been important in regulating private businesses, especially public utilities and transportation companies. Although such concerns are frequently regulated by the federal government as well, many utilities have purely intrastate operations which are regulated by state public service commissions. The efficacy of such regulation immediately concerns the utilities and their customers. In some states, the commissions allow a 10 per cent return on the utilities' investments; in others, they permit only 6 per cent. Bus and truck companies are also regulated by such commissions and must obtain consent for their tariff rates and routes; in addition, they must abide by the safety regulations which many commissions impose.

States are responsible for a host of other regulations. State departments of agriculture help protect the dominant crop of the state from unfair marketing practices, from adulteration, and from other unacceptable practices. Thus, Wisconsin's department is very concerned about its dairy industry and those in North Carolina and Virginia seek to help tobacco growers. Air and water pollution controls are being initiated in a growing number of states. Thus, state agencies require industrial polluters to install expensive treatment plants. To help control air pollution, California has not only pressured industry to install smoke-abating devices but also has forced the state's motorists to install devices on their automobiles to decrease the amount of noxious exhaust gas. Where mining is an important activity, the state is likely to have a role in inspecting mines and enforcing safety regulations.

A more obscure form of regulation, but one which also has great impact on the lives of many citizens, is that imposed on a large number of trades and professions. In most cases, this regulation has been sought by the affected occupation in order to win state support for the protection of its own as well as the public's interest. The medical profession is regulated by the state and sometimes uses this regulatory power to restrict the entry of nonresident physicians. Integrated bar associations help maintain professional discipline but also assist lawyers in their struggle to prevent others (especially accountants and real estate brokers) from engaging in what lawyers consider to be their own work. Barbers, beauticians, plumbers, and others in similar trades often have won state protection through licensing boards which help to restrict entry into these fields and thus limit competition.

Another type of regulatory activity focuses on political activities. Each state has laws regulating party organization or campaign practices. The requirements for candidacy and election themselves are stipulated by public law. The activities of interest groups are also regulated in many states. These kinds of regulations attract a different level of public attention than do those of economic interests. The extent and efficacy of their application vary greatly from state to state.

Finally, each state plays a significant role in the formulation and enforcement of criminal laws. The very definition of what is criminal is a major decision for every state legislature each session. Each state has a system of courts, at least partly financed by the state governments, to try accused offenders of these statutes. Each state has a prison system. An increasing number of states provide technical assistance to local police to help in the apprehension of violators.

Although every state engages in most of these regulatory activities (as well as others not mentioned here), the quality of such regulation varies enormously. In some states, water pollution control has been relatively effective for a number of years; in others, it is an almost untried program. In some states ostensible control over certain industries has been perverted by these industries in order to use government power to attain their private ends. Mining companies, for instance, are rarely effectively controlled—either in their safety programs, or in their strip-mining activities which denude the countryside. The oil industry, in most states where oil production is significant, has won state approval of its self-regulatory practices so that orders to produce only a certain amount of oil in a particular month have the sanction of state law. The same is true of agricultural interests in many states. What appears on the surface to be a far-reaching program of state regulation of innumerable industries is, in fact, self-regulation by the industries under the cloak of a government agency.

This brief review of the activities (outputs) of state governments demonstrates the variety of programs and the differences in emphasis that exists from state to state. With respect to each activity, state legislatures have some opportunity to affect the characteristics of the program. They must authorize the program, pass on annual (or biennial) appropriations, and approve changes in the laws affecting the program. The manner in which state legislatures do these things varies from one state to another and is the concern of the remaining chapters of this book. Before we can evaluate the significance of such variations, however, we need to examine other factors that may affect the programs of state governments. In the end, we will want to hazard some guesses as to whether the characteristics of the states themselves or the characteristics of state legislatures, are more important in influencing the outputs of state political systems.

To accomplish this objective we need to examine the remaining elements of state political systems as illustrated in Figure 1. Each has a somewhat different value in the several states and plays a somewhat different role in determining the outputs of the system.

The Environment

RESOURCES

The wealth of a state's citizens is perhaps the most influential element of the environment, even though it is relatively remote from the legislature's daily activities. Wealth is important because it provides a state with the resources for ambitious government programs and because it is likely to structure the nature of demands for particular programs. Repeated research in recent years by Glen W. Fisher, Seymour Sacks, and Robert Harriss, and James Robinson and Richard Dawson has indicated that per capita income and median family income are the best predictors of state expenditures. Furthermore, we know from other research that income relates highly with other characteristics of the population that are likely to have political significance. The wealthier the population, the higher its level of education and the more likely it is to be engaged in white-collar occupations. Both higher education and higher status jobs usually lead to greater political participation. Moreover, greater wealth, education, and participation are positively associated with a higher degree of party competition. One need not be a Marxist to acknowledge the pervading influence of wealth on social and political affairs.

Another element of a state's economy is more difficult to measure but also has an important role—the kind of economic activity that predominates in a state. Very few states are still basically agricultural—that description perhaps fits only the Dakotas, although even they have well over half their work force engaged in non-agricultural pursuits and derive far less than half of the states' personal income from agricultural pursuits. Some states are clearly dependent on a few industries: in Michigan, it is the automobile industry; in Louisiana, it is the gas, oil, and petrochemical industry; in Montana, until recently, it was copper; in Delaware, the chemical industry. In such states, as Harmon Zeigler has argued in *Politics in the American States,* politics often revolves about the interests of the dominant industry or corporation. Such industries are often reputed to "control" the state government although when we examine each case more closely, we usually find that the interest has only enough power to be heard, not to determine the outcome of each particular struggle. States with a single, dominant interest produce visibly different political forces than states with a variety of interests.

GEOGRAPHIC FACTORS

The geography of a state also plays a visible role in setting the political scene. Terrain may make some programs, such as highway construction, inordinately expensive. It may separate centers of population by formidable natural barriers which influence the structure of political interaction, despite modern communication devices. The distribution of natural resources may make one part of the state dependent upon and hostile toward another portion; this is true in California, where the northern portion of the state has the water that southern Californians desperately need. Forbidding ecological conditions may result in the concentration of a state's population in a handful of urban centers, as is true in Arizona and Nevada. The importance of the Mississippi River has long been recognized in states like Louisiana and Mississippi where the commerce generated by the river and the agriculture made possible by it have long set the delta counties apart from the rest of the state. Despite modern contrivances, such geographical features still play a major role in structuring economic and social affairs and political conflict.

SOCIAL CHARACTERISTICS OF THE POPULATION

There are many other characteristics in addition to those already mentioned. People have various ethnic backgrounds; they belong to different religions; they are of different ages. Each of these, and their derivative characteristics, have in other periods had a profound impact on American politics. Ethnic background is still a significant factor in the politics of a few states. Former immigrant group identifications still play a highly visible role in the northeastern states. Negroes as an ethnic group are performing an increasingly active role in all states where they constitute a significant minority. Religious affiliation, however, is becoming less important because of the fading of the prejudices and fears about minority religions which were widespread in the century following 1850. Age groups potentially are significant in politics but they are so evenly distributed among the various states that, with the possible exception of Florida, no state is significantly different from any other state in this regard.

POLITICAL TRADITIONS AND CULTURE

Although wealth, the dominant economic activity, geographical factors, and other social characteristics are significant, their specific impact on politics is shaped by the nature of the political tradition of each state. Economic and social conditions must be interpreted through the perceptions of participants in the political system to have an influence on politics. These perceptions are affected by the political culture of each state.

It is difficult to define precisely what we mean by political culture. For the present purpose we mean the *dominant* attitudes and values which mold political behavior.

In the United States, these cultural traits can be described in terms of sectionalism, in terms of the residues of particular political movements which swept through some states, in terms of public morality, and in terms of the styles of political leadership which seem to be acceptable and prevalent in the states.

Sectionalism. Historically, sectionalism has been the most important distinguishing trait on the American political scene. Various sections of the country have had different economic interests; they were settled by people with somewhat different backgrounds; and the physical environment produced rather different demands for governmental services. The Puritan ancestry of New England and its commercial economic base, the hot climate of the South and its cotton economy, the limitless opportunity of the Far West frontier states, the dependence on agriculture of the Middle West—each of these factors fostered a somewhat different set of political attitudes. However, by the middle of the twentieth century, almost all sectional differences are fast disappearing, even in the South.

As the South becomes more highly industrialized, wealthier, and better integrated with the rest of the country through population exchanges, its distinctive attitudes and political practices are mitigating. The civil rights movement and pressure for change slowly generated by the federal government have been important in this change, but we must remember that the civil rights movement had its genesis in the South, not in the North. It sought aid and comfort from Northern sentiment but it was born from the changes that were occurring independently in the old South and which were slowly eroding the Southern political culture.

Despite the symptoms of change, the South retains a distinctive political culture. Its traditional pattern of legal, social, and political segregation and discrimination has not yet entirely disappeared. Neither has the low level of public services provided by state governments (associated strongly with the poverty of most southern states) disappeared. The combination of poverty, the emotionally explosive issue of segregation (the "Southern way of life"), and a surviving tinge of Populism have also produced in the South more frequent resort to demagoguery than in most parts of the country. Such names as Theodore Bilbo, Albert (Happy) Chandler, Huey P. Long, and George Wallace connote a style of leadership that is seldom found elsewhere—colorful, flamboyant, little concerned with niceties, and often productive of liberal economic programs at the same time that civil liberties are little respected.

The Residue of Political Movements. In the same way as Southern politics was for a long time affected by the residue of attitudes and socio-economic conditions fostered by the Civil War, a few other states have remained under the spell of a different heritage. Perhaps the most important of these residues comes from the reform-progressive era of the first two decades of the twentieth century. Spurred by muckraking accounts of corruption in city and state government, reformers effectively changed the institutions of many states and permanently affected their political style. In New York under Theodore Roosevelt and Charles Evans Hughes, in Wisconsin under Robert LaFollette, in California under Hiram Johnson, and in Oregon under William S. U'Ren, the movement eventually produced civil service reforms, tighter regulation of lobbies, the initiative and referendum, and the direct primary. In each of these states, the reformer-progressives were organized as a separate party or as the dominant faction of one of the major parties. In each of them, social welfare legislation accompanied governmental reform. And in each there remains a resistance to corruption and a receptivity to innovation that is rarely found elsewhere in the nation. Other states were also affected by the reform-progressive movement but with fewer lasting effects. Both Illinois and Missouri elected reform governors but corruption eventually crept back into the mainstream of political life through metropolitan political machines. Even in New York, the reform movement is regularly challenged by the bosses of New York City who have never been entirely dethroned nor deprived of their statewide political influence.

Leadership Styles. The styles of political leadership that have emerged as a result of the interaction between political movements and the state's economic and social base are another important element of a state's political culture. We can distinguish different leadership styles in terms of the position from which leadership is asserted, the social origins of leadership, its mass appeal, and its ethical bounds.

In most states leadership has been traditionally asserted from the governor's office. As chief executive of the state, most governors occupy the strongest position from which leadership may be asserted. In a few states, however, other positions more frequently are the platform of leadership. In Illinois, the mayor of Chicago is often more influential than the governor. The same was true of Mayor Frank Hague of Jersey City during the 1930s and 1940s. In still other states, political leadership comes from the chief of a state or urban political machine who himself does not always hold a high state office. Virginia's politics has, for instance, been dominated by the Byrd machine for forty years. In the 1930s, Tom Pendergast similarly dominated Missouri politics. Finally, a few states traditionally have no dominant leadership. South Carolina, with its strongly localized patterns of politics, comes closest to maintaining this pattern year after year, although Missouri, since Pendergast, has also seen no strong leadership from either the governor, mayor, machine boss, or legislator.

The social origins of leadership and its mass appeal are often related. In New York, members of the social and economic elite have regularly sought and won gubernatorial office in the twentieth century. They have produced a pattern of responsible, nationally oriented, moderately liberal leadership. In many states, this elite remains aloof from elective politics. Men of more humble origin win high office. Their leadership may also be vigorous, but it is less often independent of special interests. Finally, a number of states have been governed by flamboyant demagogues. Demagogic leadership seems to flourish best in poverty-stricken social environments when an emotional issue is available, and often attracts as its leader someone who has risen rapidly from near the bottom of the social ladder. These conditions were found in Louisiana in the 1920s, Arkansas in the 1950s, and Alabama in the 1960s. Indeed, almost all recent demagogues in American state politics have been Southerners.

Political style involves more than leadership patterns. It also involves differing boundaries of propriety. Practices condoned as normal in some states would raise an outcry of public indignation in others. Louisiana, for instance, was one of the few states in the early 1960s that still deposited its funds in banks without drawing interest on them; at least one of the banks was a business venture controlled by the governor's friends and partisans. In the 1960s, Illinois and Massachusetts apparently followed practices as equally questionable as those of Louisiana. In some states, corruption is localized in metropolitan political machines; this seems to be true for recent administrations in Colorado and Pennsylvania. Moreover, even where state administrations are generally free of questionable practices, certain state enterprises are much more susceptible to corruption than others. In New York this was recently the case in the administration of liquor licenses and supervision of race tracks, functions that are often associated with corruption in other states.

Such political traditions as we have mentioned do much to give differential meaning to poverty and wealth, and to the domination by one industry or another. These traditions cause states as unlike as California and Wisconsin, and Louisiana and Massachusetts, to resemble each other in their political behavior. They cause states with rather similar socioeconomic conditions—like Illinois and Missouri, and Louisiana and Texas—to behave quite differently.

Demands for Governmental Action

Differing political traditions—combined with differing socio-economic conditions—do much to promote a variety of political demands in the fifty states.

The most marked difference among the fifty states is the extent to which certain demands are considered legitimate in some states but not in others. This is most apparent in the demands of the civil rights movement for full citizenship for Negro residents of southern states. Their right to vote, to serve on juries, to obtain justice in the courts, to hold office, and to enjoy other benefits of citizenship were until recently more seriously challenged in certain southern states than elsewhere.

With this exception, however, demands for public services and governmental programs are more alike than they are different among the states. There is an almost uniform general demand for educational opportunities, for adequate health and welfare programs, for well constructed highways, for intra-urban transportation systems, for parklands and recreational areas, for conservation of water, wildlife, and soil. Differences in the demand-structure from state to state are apparently more closely related to the composition of the population and the characteristics of the environment than to peculiar regional or state cultures. This is simply another way of saying that the national, American political culture is now dominant over parochial cultures and plays the leading role in defining for citizens what they seek from their governments.

Since the states do differ in the composition of their population and in their environmental characteristics, the level of services demanded in each state varies somewhat. The vast expanses of some of our western states require proportionately greater per capita expenditures for highways than do the smaller, more densely populated areas of the northeastern states. The extreme climatic conditions of Southern California, for example, have generated a great awareness and foresight in planning water conservation and reservoir development; in other states, only more recent droughts have generated a similar awareness and demand. The vast metropolitan complex of the northeastern states has made their residents acutely concerned with mass transportation systems, a need that is perceived as much less pressing by most of the rest of the country.

Communication of Demands

Socio-economic conditions, political traditions, and the demands for governmental services have little impact on government unless they are felt by those who make governmental decisions. The officials who compose state legislatures, executive agencies, and the courts must know of popular demands and the conditions out of which they arise before they can react to them.

It is a hallmark of American politics that there are many ways in which demands can be communicated to decision-making authorities. Traditionally, the press has played a significant role in arousing interest and passions, in spotlighting needs, and in making demands in what the publisher thinks is "the public interest." More recently, the dispossessed and those who feel left out of the political arena have rediscovered the effectiveness of mass demonstrations for voicing their demands. Rallies, marches, and sit-in demonstrations, as well as petitions, have been revived as frequently used devices for communicating demands. Nevertheless, the most common means of communicating demands in the American political system remains the political party and interest group. Every state has an intricate set of party and interest group organizations whose principal function is to communicate general or specific demands to particular decision makers. The manner in which these organizations operate are an important variable in state politics.

POLITICAL PARTIES

Every state has a Democratic and Republican party—but this fact can be extremely misleading. Although the labels are the same throughout the fifty states, the policy preferences associated with those labels have quite distinctively local connotations. In New York, most Republicans are liberal or moderate in the Dewey-Rockefeller tradition. In Arizona, the bearers of the same party label are extremely conservative, in the spirit of Barry Goldwater and J. Bracken Lee. The same holds true for Democrats. The conservative Democrats of the Byrd machine in Virginia have little except their label in common with the liberal Democrats of California and Massachusetts. A great variety of goals and preferences which the several state parties seek to promote are obscured by these common labels.

Another misleading characteristic of state parties is their apparent organization. As the party label is to be found in every state, the naive observer might assume that parties in every state are fairly well organized. The opposite is nearer the truth. In many states, parties are as fleeting a phenomenon as on the national scene—emerging from hibernation only at each election. The reasons that state party organizations are so weak are multifold, but much of the blame can be laid to the changes promoted by earlier generations of reformers. As V. O. Key, Jr. demonstrated in his *American State Politics,* the establishment of primary elections undermined party strength in state after state. Party organization no longer had the same purpose, nor attracted the ambitious, because it could not serve as the vehicle for promotion to higher office. Party organizations found themselves forced to support whichever candidates were nominated at the primary election. Moreover, candidates usually discovered that they had to construct their own electoral machines in order to win the primary, because the party organization was supposedly prohibited from participating in primary elections. Thus, candidates often developed their personal, factional organizations and the political party itself in many places became a hollow shell.

Other reforms also contributed to organizational weakness. Most states minutely regulate party structure in order to minimize boss manipulation. Such legislation, in fact, does not completely avoid the danger of boss domination, but it has paralyzed parties by requiring them to work with an unwieldy, inflexible organizational structure. Most party organizations are governed by large conventions of delegates elected at the precinct or ward level, of convention stacked upon convention from the county, through a district, to the state level, or composed of a combination of elected officials and party committeemen who have little in common. The exact shape of the strait-jacket in which state party organizations are bound varies considerably from state to state, but a strait-jacket it remains. In California and Wisconsin, organizational paralysis has been partly overcome by the establishment of extralegal party organizations —volunteer groups that perform all the functions of the legal party but which escape the statutory regulations from which the legal party suffers. In those states, the legal party organizations do little more than meet as often as state law requires; all other functions are performed by the volunteer groups.

A third cause for the weakness of state party organizations is that party finances are strictly controlled in many states. As Alexander Heard indicated in *The Costs of Democracy,* such regulation of campaign contributions and expenditures has promoted the profusion of campaign committees at election time and the fragmentation (instead of centralization) of party organization. Just as the direct primary law prevents state parties from controlling the nomination of candidates, so campaign finance laws prevent parties from controlling the financing of election campaigns.

There are other causes for the weakness of state parties. In some states, the strong tradition of localism has resisted all efforts to centralize party organization, as it has resisted the centralization of other political efforts. The fact that most statewide officials run separately rather than on a combined ticket, that the governor's term is usually more limited than that of other officials, and that metropolitan offices are sometimes more attractive (and powerful) than state offices—all these help to weaken the statewide party organization.

Nevertheless, there are important variations in the strength of the state-wide party, and these appear to be significantly related to the degree of party competition. Where competition between the Democratic and Republican parties is the keenest, party organization appears to be strongest. Where either the Democratic or Republican parties predominate, party organization is usually most fragile and local or factional groups within the parties are the strongest.

The measurement of party competition is no simple task, as competition may occur or be absent at any of the many elections held each quadrennium. One measure which takes into account a number of different state elections has been devised by James Robinson, Richard Dawson, and Austin Ranney. They have computed the average per cent of the popular vote won by the gubernatorial candidates of each party, the average per cent of the seats in the state senate and state assembly held by each party, and the per cent of all gubernatorial terms during which the same party controlled both houses of the legislature as well as the governor's office. Averaging these percentages provides a measure by which we may rank the states from those in which the Democratic party has predominated, to those in which the two parties are fairly evenly matched, to those in which the Republican party is strongest. The results for 1946-63 are shown in Table 1.

The index scores indicate the average per cent of domination by the Democratic party. Thus, South Carolina had unbroken Democratic domination during this period; Georgia, Louisiana, Mississippi, Texas, Alabama, Arkansas, and Florida, in that order, followed closely behind. In each of these states, the Republican party was completely unsuccessful in winning significant contests in *state* elections. It did win important national elections—such as Senator Tower's seat in the United States Senate, and a majority or plurality of votes for Republican presidential candidates. Such successes on the national scene, however, were not paralleled in the state political arena.

The table also shows that Republicans were not as strong in their strongest states as the Democrats were in the Democratic states. In no state did the Republicans shut out the Democrats as the Democrats had shut out the Republicans in South Carolina. The strongest Republican state was about equivalent to Oklahoma on the Democratic side, the twelfth state from the most Democratic extreme.

The absence of totally Republican states, and the increasing demonstrations of Republican strength in the deep South, point to a growth of two-party competition within the states. Most states now have had relatively even party competition over the span of a decade, with both Democrats and Republicans enjoying a good chance of winning the governor's office and one or both houses of the state legislature. This is most true for states in the middle of the scale—Delaware, Nevada, Massachusetts, Hawaii, Colorado, Montana, Minnesota, and Utah. Even states that on

Table 1: Interparty Competition in the Fifty States, 1946-63

(Most Democratic)					Index Scores				(Most Republican)
1.00-.90	.89-.80	.79-.70	.69-.60	.59-.50	.49-.40	.39-.30	.29-.20	.19-.10	.09-.00
S.C.	Va.	Ky.	Alaska	Wash.	Hawaii	Calif.	Wis.	N.D.	Vt.
Ga.	N.C.	Ariz.	Mo.	Del.	Colo.	Neb.	N.H.		
La.	Tenn.	W. Va.	R.I.	Nev.	Mont.	Ill.	Iowa		
Miss.	Okla.	Md.		Mass.	Minn.	Idaho	Kans.		
Tex.		N.M.			Utah	Mich.	Me.		
Ala.					Conn.	N.J.	S.D.		
Ark.					Pa.	Ind.			
Florida						Ore.			
						Ohio			
						Wyo.			
						N.Y.			

Source: Austin Ranney, "Parties in State Politics," in Politics in the American States, eds. Herbert Jacob and Kenneth N. Vines. Boston: Little, Brown, 1965, p. 65.

the scale seem fairly distant from the most competitive ones, however, have in recent years experienced quite fierce competition, so that their scale position reflects more of their past history than present experience. That is particularly true of Wisconsin where, in 1958, Democrats broke a long period of Republican domination; New York, which seems precariously balanced between Democrats and Republicans; and Oklahoma, where Republicans won the governorship in 1962.

The growth of competition may be further accelerated by legislative reapportionment. Legislative reapportionment seems to be favoring Democrats in some northern states in so far as it makes it possible for them to win that house of the legislature which had previously been reserved for rural interests, which normally were Republican. This seems to have been an important factor in enabling the Democrats to win control of the Michigan Senate in 1964 and to win majorities in both houses of the New Jersey legislature in 1965.

INTEREST GROUPS

Interest groups perform many of the same functions that parties do, but in quite different ways. Parties channel popular demands to the government through their role in selecting candidates for public office, by their exposition of policy alternatives in platforms and campaigns, and by their influence on decisions in legislatures and in executive agencies. Parties seek to attract as wide an adherence as possible, at least until they have won a secure majority of the electorate. Interest groups are also concerned with channelling the desires of the public to its government, but each group operates in a much more restricted sphere than the Democratic or Republican parties do. Interest groups are primarily concerned with influencing decisions, and only secondarily, when at all, with selecting decision makers. Interest groups have a narrow base of support; they seek adherents among all those who share a narrow concern—dairymen, truckers, railroads, distillers, brewers, veterans, parents, etc. —rather than a broad base among the general public.

The principal purpose of many groups is to present particular demands to appropriate public agencies, to help their membership in dealing directly with the government, and to give their membership information about government services and activities that affect them. Groups retain their membership in large part as a result of their efficiency in these operations. Unlike parties whose influence has been progressively restricted to elective officials by the growth of civil service, interest groups perform these functions among appointed as well as elected officials. Their activity is perhaps most visible in the lobbies of the state legislature, but many groups do their most important work inside the offices of administrative and regulatory agencies. Truckers, for instance, are not simply concerned with legislation that sets length and weight limits; they are also concerned with the specifications for new highways, their routing, and the highway department's administration of statutory standards. Teachers are not just concerned with legislation; they are equally interested in the administrative decisions of state officials regarding certification requirements, curricula, text books, building standards, and the myriad of other decisions which flow from the state's educational agency. Indeed, the principal purpose of some groups is to bring about the establishment of special agencies for their clientele—boards to regulate barbers, beauticians, engineers, pharmacists, plumbers, and the like. Once such boards have been established, the occupational interest group's primary activity is likely to consist of appearances before that board and of activity within it so that private desires can be translated into governmental decisions.

Such interest group activity is also of great value for many government officials. It is particularly useful to legislators who seek information about a subject on which they are not expert, for which they have no assistance to procure expert information, but which a group can furnish them *gratis*. Administrators typically are less dependent on groups for specialized data since most agencies have their own expert staffs. Nevertheless, groups perform an equally vital although different function for many administrative agencies. They provide channels of communication between the agency and its clientele so the agency can better know how its proposals will be received, what support (or opposition) they may arouse, and what changes in the proposals are necessary in order to win legislative (or gubernatorial) approval.

The range and number of interest groups varies greatly from state to state. Unfortunately, we do not possess as much reliable information, even purely formal information, about groups as we do about parties. Among seventeen states for which comparable information is available, according to Harmon Zeigler, the number of groups registered with the state ranges from a low of 41 in Kansas to a high of 439 in Florida. Not only do the number of registered groups differ a great deal from state to state, but also their distribution among various interests varies. In all states the largest number of groups represent business. In some, business representation is largely through trade associations, while in others most of the representation is by single business firms which engage their own lobbyists, or whose owners act as lobbyists. For instance, in Kentucky, most registered business lobbyists are trade associations; in Virginia, almost all of them are individual firms. There are other important differences. In some states, labor is represented by a few lobbyists; in others, each union seems to have its own representative. In some states, no religious or veterans groups have registered; in other states, they are officially represented.

Mere numbers, of course, are not an accurate indication of strength. A single group that has the united support of an important interest is stronger than a dozen groups fighting among each other over the right to represent an occupation or industry. Therefore, we have to examine the conditions under which interest groups are strong and the circumstances under which they are weak.

Groups acquire strength from their internal arrangements and their relationship with the political system. Thus groups with considerable financial resources, a united and intensely concerned membership, an effective leadership, and a limited set of narrowly defined issues on which they work are likely to be quite strong. In addition, if a group of this kind is located in a state where it has a recognized claim to influence governmental decisions, its strength will be greatly increased. Most groups, however, lack maximum strength because they do not enjoy all of these characteristics. Some groups are strong in one state and weak in others because they are considered more legitimate in the former; this is particularly true of labor unions and civil rights groups. Further, groups that play a more important part in the economic life of the state are likely to be more influential than those that play a peripheral role. Thus, farmers' groups are likely to be most important in agricultural states and much less so in industrialized ones; automobile manufacturers are an extremely significant interest in Michigan but scarcely noticeable in the other states.

Although the influence of a particular group is important in tracing the fate of particular policy proposals, the political system of a state is shaped more by the effectiveness of interest groups as a whole than by that of a single group. The role that interest groups play is related to the strength of political parties and the economic base of the state. According to Harmon Zeigler's study of state interest groups, where parties are effectively organized and in constant competition with each other, interest groups play a lesser role than in states where parties are weaker. In addition, where economic activity is relatively concentrated in a handful of dominant industries, these industries and related interest groups will dominate the interest-group process. States with highly diversified economies also have more diversified interest-group processes. Focusing on the strength of parties and the economic base of a state, Zeigler identifies four interest-group patterns among the states: 1) alliance of dominant groups, as in Maine; 2) a single dominant interest, as Anaconda Copper was formerly in Montana; 3) conflict between two dominant interests, as in Michigan between auto manufacturers and auto workers' unions; and 4) the "triumph" of many interests, as in California.

Nonlegislative Decision-Making Institutions

The demands carried by parties, interest groups, and the other channels of communication flow to particular decision-making institutions. Some can be satisfied only by legislation; others can be more appropriately resolved by executive or judicial agencies. Each of the three branches of government, however, participates to some extent in the

other's work. Each also has certain structural characteristics that affect
the output decisions of the political system.

In the following chapters the peculiar characteristics of state legislatures will be examined in some detail. At this point we need to look at
the characteristics of executive and judicial agencies in order to understand how they may serve as alternatives to the legislature and how their
structural characteristics affect output decisions.

EXECUTIVE AGENCIES

The organization of the executive branch varies considerably from
state to state. Each state has approximately the same set of major officials
but they serve under quite different conditions. This is particularly true
of the governor. Some governors may serve as long as the electorate wishes,
winning four-year terms each time; at the opposite end of the scale, the
governors of New Mexico and South Dakota, for example, may serve only
two two-year terms—if they can win them.

In most states the governor is not the only statewide elected official.
Frequently, the attorney general, state treasurer, secretary of state, state
auditor, as well as the lieutenant governor are elected independently of
the governor; these officials are often allowed to serve longer than the
governor. In addition, more than half the states elect a superintendent
of schools; in a few others, heads of the agriculture department, insurance
department, tax commission, highway department, and some miscellaneous departments are also elected independently. The consequence of this
situation is that in many states the governor is not chief executive in the
style of the President; rather, he is one of many executives.

In addition, most governors labor in an administrative maze of appointed officials who staff what appear to be subordinate agencies that
fall under the governor's formal control. In many states, there are more
than two dozen such agencies operating important programs; there are
many more which regulate a particular trade, occupation, industry, or
profession. Although these agencies are nominally under the governor's
control, he cannot effectively coordinate their activities; indeed, he may
have difficulty discovering what they are doing. Consequently, a large
number of agencies lead their own lives beyond the pale of effective
gubernatorial direction or control. They develop close relationships with
clientele interest groups; they try to obtain what they need from the
legislature without much gubernatorial intervention. In five states (Indiana, North Carolina, Rhode Island, Tennessee, and West Virginia)
the governor has such weak veto powers (in North Carolina he has none)
that he may be almost entirely bypassed by agencies nominally under his
control when they seek legislative action. The major consequence of the
executive disorganization rampant in many states is that political effort is
so fragmented as to defy control or even systematic description. The gov-

ernor often lacks the power to avert failure, although he may be blamed for it.

THE JUDICIARY

Courts are the third branch of government to which demands for action may flow. State courts, however, principally handle complaints about the violation of criminal laws and complaints about the violation of private agreements. Most of these complaints are handled by a quasi-administrative process: a guilty plea in criminal cases and an out-of-court settlement or uncontested hearing in civil proceedings. Such cases almost never raise policy issues that concern other branches of government.

On occasion, however, a dispute is brought to the courts instead of the legislature because the legislature would not entertain it or would not satisfy the demands being made. Such actions arise in the form of challenges to the constitutionality of a statute or its interpretation by an executive official. In such cases the decisions of the courts have a direct impact on the legislature and are significant to the political system. For instance, since the United States Supreme Court decided that abuses of the legislature's power to apportion its seats may be challenged in court, state as well as federal courts have played the leading role in forcing reapportionment of state legislatures, sometimes pressuring the legislatures to act and sometimes formulating the apportionment scheme themselves. Other occasions also arise for state courts to participate in public policy making. Courts respond to complaints about the fairness of administrative procedures, issue injunctions against public agencies, and decide claims against them.

Nevertheless, courts play a much less important role in the political system than legislatures and executive agencies. Few "public" demands are channelled to the courts; and they make relatively few policy or program decisions. The manner in which they administer justice may have very significant consequences for the stability of the system in the long run, but in the short run their handling of "private" complaints and disputes has little consequence for the system or for other governmental agencies.

Boundaries

All political systems have boundaries within which they operate. These boundaries greatly influence what actions occur in the political arena. They are never entirely constant or stable. Part of the conflict that is normal in a political system is the struggle to maintain, extend, or retract the boundaries of the system.

The boundaries exist on at least two levels. The first defines what is properly the scope of *political* action; that is, what any political system

may do. The second defines what is within the scope of the *state* political
system as contrasted to the national and local political systems.

The limits on political action are typically contained in constitutional
provisions in the United States. The Bill of Rights and other amendments of the national constitution, and the parallel portions of state
constitutions, prohibit governmental action in certain spheres. Thus,
American governments are prohibited, for instance, from inhibiting free-
dom of religion; they may not take life, liberty, or property without due
process of law; they may not prohibit voting by women. Such guarantees
—and there are many more of them—are of course not crystal clear. They
are constantly interpreted by the courts and by other government agencies.
But they represent the civil liberties that are considered inviolate by many
Americans and which neither state nor other governments may ordinarily
trespass.

The second category of boundaries defines the functions that may be
performed by the state systems and by national or local political systems.
Some guidelines are contained in the national and state constitutions.
The national constitution gives the federal government control over
foreign relations, interstate commerce, coinage of money, operation of
the postal services, declaration of war, and the other functions mentioned
in Section 8 of Article I. Consequently, unless Congress does not use its
powers or explicitly authorizes state action, the states are excluded from
these functions. Likewise, state constitutions often define the powers of
local governments: cities, counties, and special districts. Constitutionally,
these governments are subordinate to the state but many constitutions
guarantee some of them a measure of "home rule" through which they
may autonomously decide their own policies with little or no interference
from the state.

The boundaries between national, state, and local political systems,
however, are not mortar walls which precisely separate one system from
another. Rather, all these systems coexist within the same geographic
boundaries; they share many functions with each other. The state systems
are in intricate balance between the national and local systems. Much of
state politics revolves about decisions on how to structure these intergovernmental relations—whether to yield to a particular local demand,
whether to accept a federal grant, whether to request additional federal
help, or whether to maintain a greater degree of autonomy. In popular
terms, these conflicts are often identified as controversies about states'
rights and home rule.

FEDERAL-STATE RELATIONS

The federal and state systems share many important functions. The
states play a fundamental role in constituting the national government.
They control the elections at which congressmen, senators, and presidential electors are chosen. In turn, the federal government plays an im-

portant supportive role in financing and supervising programs that are largely administered by the states, such as those for highway construction, welfare, and education.

The federal government participates in these programs principally by helping the states finance them and by setting conditions for the acceptance of such help. In the sphere of transportation, the federal government has played this role ever since its promotion of public roads in the early nineteenth century. In the middle of the twentieth century it is providing most of the funds for interstate highway construction; in return it imposes materiel and labor standards and supervises the routing of highways. Welfare programs are also now largely under the supervision of the federal government, although this is a development dating only from the New Deal. Many of the states' responsibilities in the field of welfare have been taken over entirely by the federal government through the Social Security system. Other programs, such as Aid for Families with Dependent Children (formerly A.D.C.), are largely financed by the federal government but administered by the states. The only large-scale one remaining almost completely under state control is the general assistance program which helps those who are not covered by any of the others.

In education, the federal government has played a leading but only intermittent role for many years. Its grants of land under the Morrill Act of 1862 were of fundamental significance in propelling public higher education in America toward its present position of eminence. Later grants financed vocational training in public schools and promoted scientific education. Until the aid to education programs passed under the Johnson Administration, however, federal participation in education remained limited to intermittent grants or highly specialized programs. With the Johnson Administration's programs adopted in 1965, the federal government began to play an increasingly important role in financing and controlling public education at all levels.

The impact on the states of this shared responsibility with the national government is multifold. In the six-year period between 1960 and 1966, it is estimated by the federal government that federal aid to state and local governments almost doubled from $7.2 billion to $13.6 billion. Most of this aid is concentrated in three programs: highways, welfare, and education. The amount being spent by the federal government for education is growing rapidly. Before the new programs of the Johnson Administration, it was giving only $405 million to the states and localities for education; the estimate for the second year of the Johnson program was for aid totalling more than $1.3 billion, a three-fold increase.

The influx of federal funds is a boon to the poorer states. It has enabled them to close the gap significantly between their own welfare programs and those of wealthier states. But the federal money carries requirements with it. Accepting federal funds may mean committing large sums of state money since almost all the grants require matching funds from the state treasury. Thus, decisions made in Washington have an immediate and large-scale impact on the budgets of the fifty states. Unless a state is willing to forego the federal largesse—and that happens only rarely—the state must earmark whatever funds the federal government determines.

Federal aid has other consequences as well. It has effectively turned the attention of groups seeking new programs from the state capitals to Washington, for although congressional approval is not easy to win, once obtained it immediately affects the whole nation; to go to the state capitals for similar approval means fifty independent efforts. Consequently, much of the pressure for innovation and experimentation is now exerted in Washington rather than in the states. Innovative programs and policies appear at the national rather than state level.

Without doubt, there have been important costs in the centralization of financing and in the increasing participation of the national government in domestic programs. For instance, it appears that the 1965 Highway Beautification Act quite unintentionally stymied the independent action of the state governments to achieve the same end but by different legal means. Wisconsin, for instance, found it necessary to suspend its own program for removing highway signs along interstate routes because if it continued, it would lose large sums of money in its highway grants. Instead, it had to wait for the national government to institute its own, more expensive program. Thus, an innovative state is penalized for having taken the initiative in a program that was eventually administered by the national government.

The establishment of federal standards and restrictions also has many consequences for the states. It restricts their scope of policy making. State legislatures are confronted with a severely limited set of choices rather than having a relatively free hand to develop policy. Federal standards in some fields have required extensive changes in state government. Thanks to federal welfare legislation, all states have at least some of their employees under civil service and have organized their welfare programs so that they meet federal standards. Professionals are required for certain highway jobs because of federal standards. Many states had such standards before federal legislation; others were forced to adopt them or lose their grants.

According to most observers, the trend toward greater national participation in state programs is likely to intensify. The states are all faced with limited financial resources and seemingly unlimited demands for public services. The federal government has a much more flexible revenue system which, according to government economists, will produce a substantial budget surplus in the late 1960s and early 1970s. It is of course possible that the federal government will simply lower its tax rates. But it has also been proposed by the former chairman of the Council of Economic Advisers, Walter Heller, that at least some of this surplus be returned to the states in the form of general grants-in-aid. Such aid would better enable the states to meet demands for new services, but would also make them increasingly dependent on the national government. It seems unlikely to this writer that markedly increased aid would long remain unaccompanied by increased federal supervision of state operations.

STATE-LOCAL RELATIONS

The formal, legal position of the states, vis-à-vis their local governments, is quite different from that of states toward the federal government. Local governments are legally subordinate to the states; they are creatures of the states and their charters can be altered or even withdrawn by the states. However, this superior legal position has been seriously eroded by the strong tradition of local home rule which exists in almost every state. Consequently, the activities of local governments create a significant boundary that restricts the decisions of state political systems.

To a considerable degree, local governments enjoy *de jure* or *de facto* home-rule powers. In many states such autonomy is guaranteed by provisions of the state constitution or by statute. Even where it is not committed to the statute books, considerable autonomy in fact exists. This autonomy is promoted by powerful lobbies at the state capital representing local government officials. Many legislators and elected state officials themselves have had some prior experience in local agencies and still enjoy contacts with local office holders in their district. These facts reinforce the strength of local governments.

In some states, the largest cities enjoy a position of pre-eminence and play a large role in state politics. Ten cities in ten different states had more than 15 per cent of their state's population in 1960. Although their share of population has been declining (while suburban areas have grown), these cities still exert considerable influence on state politics. No governor or legislature can remain indifferent to what happens in New York City or Los Angeles. The government of Chicago often seems more powerful than the state government in Springfield. Baltimore looms large in Maryland politics and Milwaukee's shadow often reaches the state capitol in Madison.

Such large cities pose a particularly difficult problem to state political systems. Election outcomes there usually determine the results of state-wide races. The budgets of these cities often approach those of the whole state government. Problems in these cities have become acute and cry for attention and resolution, even though the state may be without sufficient resources to help if it wished to—and often it is not sympathetic to the plight of a metropolitan core city. As a consequence, such cities have increasingly turned directly to the federal government for assistance. The result has been that large cities have evolved close ties with federal officials involved in housing and redevelopment and short-circuited the states. With the establishment in 1965 of the new federal Department of Housing and Urban Development, the chances are that such contacts will multiply and spread and that the states will be left out of important decisions. The war on poverty has short-circuited state officials, although local officials have also complained that their wishes have not been given enough attention.

Another consequence of large cities for state politics is that they tend to develop into centers of opposition to the state government. The governors of California, Illinois, and New York constantly fight a guerilla war with the mayors of their largest cities. It is rare that the mayors openly challenge them in elections but they often support opposing factions within the governor's party or strengthen the opposition party.

Large cities are not alone in patrolling the boundaries of state political systems. The many small and special political subdivisions of the state also produce significant limitations. As we have already seen, they make significant demands on state budgets. Theoretically, such demands would make them responsive to control by the state government. In fact, their grants are sacrosanct, fixed obligations on the states which even the most courageous governor or determined legislature cannot change or will not challenge. The lobby of these local governments operates with great effectiveness in the state capitol. Consequently, the policies governing many state programs are shaped by the fact that they are carried out by these autonomous units.

What Is the Combined Impact of These Systemic Characteristics?

At the present level of sophistication in the study of state politics, it is not possible to construct a precise rank-ordering of the impact of the systemic characteristics, described in this chapter, on the many decisions that are produced by state governments. It is necessary, no doubt, to distinguish among different kinds of decisions in assessing the relative importance of these characteristics. On the basis of the research that has been done, we may venture a tentative typology of outputs and a ranking of the factors that seem to affect them. Table 2 shows the major categories of outputs of state political systems and ranks the factors we have discussed.

Several qualifications must be attached to this presentation. Most important, it is simply hypothetical; it is based on the incomplete and often unsystematic literature available. Secondly, although the several types of decisions are presented in separate columns, they are not independent of each other. Thus, the decision to spend funds on non-federally aided programs is highly dependent on previous decisions to tax. Third, not all decisions of state political systems are included in the analysis. The almost innumerable conflict-settling decisions of the state judiciary are unrepresented in this figure, since most of these decisions are directed to private rather than public controversies. In the long run, the perceived justice or injustice of such decisions will have an impact on state poli-

Table 2: The Importance of Systemic Variables in the Decisions of State Governments—Some Hypothetical Rank Orderings.

Expenditure Decisions

Extractive Decisions (*e.g.*, taxation)	Programs Not Aided by Federal Government	Programs Aided by Federal Government
1. Economic base	1. Wealth	1. Wealth
2. Wealth	2. Political culture	2. Federal bounds
3. Federal bounds	3. Local bounds	3. Characteristics of governor
4. Political culture	4. Interest group characteristics	4. Political culture
5. Interest group characteristics	5. Characteristics of governor	5. Interest group characteristics
6. Characteristics of governor	6. *Characteristics of legislature*	6. Local bounds
7. Party characteristics	7. Party characteristics	7. Party characteristics
8. *Characteristics of legislature*	8. Economic base	8. *Characteristics of legislature*
9. Local bounds	9. Characteristics of judiciary	9. Economic base
10. Characteristics of judiciary	10. Federal bounds	10. Characteristics of judiciary

Regulatory Decisions

Regulation of Business	Regulation of Occupations and Professions	Regulation of Political Activities
1. Economic base	1. Interest group characteristics	1. Political culture
2. Federal bounds	2. *Characteristics of legislature*	2. *Characteristics of legislature*
3. Interest group characteristics	3. Characteristics of governor	3. Characteristics of governor
4. Political culture	4. Political culture	4. Characteristics of judiciary
5. Characteristics of judiciary	5. Economic base	5. Federal bounds
6. Characteristics of governor	6. Characteristics of judiciary	6. Party characteristics
7. Party characteristics	7. Local bounds	7. Local bounds
8. *Characteristics of legislature*	8.–10. (tied): Federal bounds; Party characteristics; Wealth	8.–10. (tied): Economic base; Interest-group characteristics; Wealth
9. Local bounds		
10. Wealth		

tics, but in the short run, no single decision is likely to have a discernible impact.

The principal conclusion to be drawn from the configuration of factors in the diagram is the relatively low ranking of legislative characteristics. Although the characteristics of state legislatures are closely related to most important decisions in state political systems, these characteristics are not likely to be as influential on the outcome as many other factors. Indeed, it is my estimation that the characteristics of state legislatures rank high only in determining regulation of occupations and professions, and in regulating political activities. Legislative characteristics rank third from the bottom in determining tax decisions, federally aided expenditures, and the regulation of business, and fifth in determining nonfederally aided expenditures.

This conclusion does not mean that legislatures are mechanical rubber stamps that could just as well be eliminated. On the contrary, they perform essential, legitimizing functions in the American scheme of government and politics. What this conclusion does mean is that details of how legislatures are organized, how they are staffed, how they do their business, exactly who becomes a legislator and how long he remains, and the rules under which he operates do not shape the outputs of a state government as significantly as does the economic base of the state (on tax decisions and business regulations), the wealth of the state (on expenditure decisions), the interest-group structure (on regulation of occupations and professions), or the political culture (on regulation of political activities).

If this diagnosis is correct, we should guard against expecting unreasonable results from formal plans to revitalize state legislatures. Such schemes will produce desirable and useful improvements; but they cannot be expected to revolutionize state politics, or grossly change the outputs of state political systems. State political systems are extraordinarily complex and the machinery of government does not solely determine the outputs of the system.

William J. Keefe

2

The Functions and Powers
of the State Legislature

The state legislature is one of the anomalies of the American political system. It has very few public supporters. Its own members sometimes turn out to be its most inflexible critics. The communications media are most likely to report its affairs when the matters at hand are bizarre or when legislators are intransigent, whether with one another or with the governor. The public reputation of the legislature with the public is seldom as good as its actual warrant to public respect. Its contributions to significant public policy are seen more often as legislative response to the initiatives of others than as legislative accomplishment. Its partisanship is perhaps as likely to be attributed to the perversity of party members as it is to the fact that legislative parties struggle over issues that count. Its independence is about as likely to be interpreted as obstinacy as it is to legislative option. Its powers seldom appear commensurate with its responsibilities. The American state legislature is an institution waning in everything except resilience.

This essay aims neither to free the legislature from opprobrium nor to add new material to the usual arraignment, although it often touches on the quality of the institution and its members. The purpose is rather to analyze the character of legislative tasks and the environments within which state legislatures maintain themselves and come to terms with the responsibilities of state government.

WILLIAM J. KEEFE *is Professor of Political Science and Chairman of the Department of Political Science at Chatham College. Professor Keefe has received two Social Science Research Council fellowships and his publications include* The American Legislative Process: Congress and the States (*with Morris Ogul*).

Main Functions of the Legislature

LAWMAKING

The burden of settling conflict and making authoritative rules for American society has always been lodged essentially within legislative jurisdiction. Any legislature, of course, may choose or be driven to delegate responsibilities which diminish its control over lawmaking, but this does not change the fact that in legal, constitutional terms lawmaking is mainly, if not purely, a legislative task. Lawmaking is by no means the only function of the state legislature but, measured by the time this activity is allotted, it is plainly the most important.

The Sources of Law. It is one thing to point out that state constitutions endow legislatures with the responsibility of making laws for the state and quite another to say that the legislature dominates the lawmaking process. The latter may be far from the case. The legislature's autonomy is virtually always under siege. Political interest groups of infinite variety, the governor and the bureaucracy, extralegislative party agencies, and individual citizens all have access to the legislature. Among those which have access are some that have great influence.

To the familiar pressures of these interests must be added the pressures of the federal government through its multiple programs that both invite and encourage state participation. The invitation to participate in federal grant-in-aid programs—involving, say, public welfare, highways, education, public health, or employment security—is overwhelmingly tempting to the typical legislature having a long list of problems that might be met through the use of federal funds. The conditions for participation in these programs are, of course, established at the national level. The effect of the matching-fund requirement is to erode legislative control over some measure of state funds; obviously, for example, money allocated to a federally sponsored highway program cannot be spent at the same time on some other program. Whatever their merit, programs carrying available money produce their own supporters. All in all, the state legislature's role in federal aid programs is less that of making law than of endorsing law already made at another level—a decision to participate is something less than the decision to initiate.

The legislative agenda itself should be viewed in the context of external pressure. The major bills on crowded legislative calendars—those which can command consideration if not always majority support—are often the work of outsiders, particularly of the governor and of administrative agencies and to a lesser extent, apparently, of private political interest groups. Seldom major in significance, the typical "legislator's bill" is designed to solve a local problem, to meet local pressure, to convey advantage to certain parochial interests, or to satisfy a pet peeve. The legislator's own bill is commonly a "merely" bill: this bill "merely" prohibits the possession of liquor in baseball parks, prohibits the operation of boats having a horsepower rating in excess of seven and one-half on this-or-that lake, or makes it unlawful to purchase lotteries or numbers tickets.

It seems unquestionably true, although the evidence is largely inferential, that bills that serve *statewide* purposes are far more likely to owe their authorship to the administration than to the creativity of some legislator or group of legislators. Legislators monitor local problems. What concerns and agitates the legislators' constituents concerns and agitates the legislators. Their preoccupation is wholly natural.

The governor's role in lawmaking varies from state to state. But the dominant pattern is clearly one of active leadership. The governor establishes the broad goals for the legislature, outlines *his* legislative program, places the stamp of urgency on certain problems, keeps "administration" bills visible to the press and various attentive publics throughout the session, and pressures the legislature to act. Not only are the major bills often of administration sponsorship, but the support for their passage may be put together by administration lobbyists. For reasons to be considered subsequently, the governor is often in name and in fact the "chief legislator" of the state. This does not make legislative leadership superfluous, but it does change its character. Legislative leaders tend to be the governor's men, chosen for their loyalty as well as their skills or followings. The governor may be directly involved in their selection.

Volume, Scope, and Impact of Legislation. Not many legislatures follow a rule of parsimony in the introduction of legislation. In recent years roughly 80,000 to 90,000 bills and resolutions have been introduced in each regular (principal) session of the fifty state legislatures. About one-third of these proposals are usually adopted. Some states approve nearly three out of every four proposals introduced, while others approve less than one out of ten.

The entire sweep of democratic experience is represented in legislation. Virtually no activity today can avoid a brush with law, a situation that leads to the enormous quantity of bills and resolutions introduced in the states. Two basic reasons account for the volume.

First, a society becoming increasingly urbanized and industrialized has great need for legislation that regulates private and public organizations and defines procedures, rights, and responsibilities. The sheer complexity of society is thus a major reason for the flood of legislation. It would be instructive, for example, to see how many bills are introduced in any typical session of a state simply to meet problems associated with the use of automobiles. The variety is staggering.

Second, governments are now the main source of many programs once handled, if at all, through private initiative. The emergence of the positive state has led to an astonishing quantity of legislation devoted to such subjects as unemployment compensation, disability, occupational diseases, public and mental health, conservation, and public welfare.

Each time a new law is added to the statutes, the possibility arises that subsequent legislatures will be required to rework it through amendments. In a word, law begets law.

Ordinarily, most bills adopted by the legislature go into effect immediately upon signature by the governor, or on a particular calendar date, or after a certain number of days following the end of the session. A few become effective on specified later days. Rarer still, the effective date may be left to administrative discretion. The notable fact, however, is that laws are turned out each session in exceptional quantities. The overwhelming majority of enactments have small beginnings and inconspicuous endings and are never reported in the press. A few major bills command virtually all of the newspaper print devoted to legislation. The bills of sharp concern to the general public commonly involve revenue, expenditures, and education.

Among the array of bills passed each session are an extraordinary number that affect only specialized interests and clienteles. The public at large is unlikely to be significantly affected by them, and indeed there is no reason why the average citizen should even be aware of their enactment. In the endless marshaling of "clientele" bills are those which provide for licensing (say, of plumbers, chiropodists, optometrists, horseshoers, boarding homes, funeral directors, barbers and beauticians, burial grounds, and liquor establishments, to mention but a few), which clarify duties, jurisdictions, and authority of administrative agencies and personnel, and which regulate specialized activities (*e.g.*, the propagation of domestic mink in captivity, the ownership of dogs by unnaturalized foreign-born residents, or the development of retirement systems for city employees). A heavy proportion of all the bills introduced and adopted are minor, amendatory bills incorporating technical changes in *existing* law. The provisions of these laws are drawn with care, usually by legislative reference services. Although these amendatory bills have general relevance for the system, they have slight relevance for the citizenry. Only a small proportion of the bills passed in any session of the legislature touch the lives of the general citizenry in an immediate and significant way. These bills, of course, may have extraordinary impacts on private and public life within the state.

REPRESENTING MULTIPLE INTERESTS

American state legislators not only are *state* representatives but are also representatives of local *constituencies* and of local and state *party organizations*. In addition, some legislators perceive themselves as steady or occasional agents of particular interest aggregations, such as agriculture, business, or labor.

Legislators represent constituencies in two ways. They do so through personal service, or errand-running, for constituents. Both the American people *and* their legislators are habituated to the notion that errand-running is an appropriate function of the legislator, one not easily set aside in favor of other tasks. Constituents have problems dealing with social security, relief, taxes, unemployment, with getting their sons and daughters into universities and colleges, with laws that affect their professions or businesses, with the rulings and practices of administrative agencies, and with any number of welfare programs. In the public's view of the job, legislators are elected to hear grievances and to listen to requests, and then to work for remedies or redress. Correspondingly, legislators see in errand-running the chance to transform necessity into opportunity. Requests are difficult to avoid in any case, and by handling them properly new support may be won for the next campaign. There are doubtless many legislatures where members spend a majority of their time handling the "casework" of their constituents.

Legislators also represent constituents by initiating and supporting legislation that confers advantages on their districts. There is scant mystery as to why members "vote the district" when relevant legislation is at stake. They are themselves district members, influenced by the district social, economic, and political environments in which they are elected. Moreover, the chances are strong that in important respects their backgrounds will resemble those of the dominant elements within their districts. The things that bind them to their districts are more important than the things that separate them. Finally, even though constituents have very little specific information concerning legislative voting records, members *believe* that their records are both visible and critical to their re-election; and in a sense this is true. Legislators deal in "increments and margins" in the electoral struggle—a few votes won or lost may prove decisive. Re-election may turn on satisfying the policy claims of certain "attentive" publics within the district which do study legislative voting records. To do less than this, in the judgment of many legislators, is to refuse to make a serious bid for power.

Legislators and constituents meet at the point where constituents ask assistance, question actions, or assert claims. Tuggings from the constituency are ever-present stimuli in the life of the legislator. How do legislators view the role of being a representative? Does concern for the constituency dominate the outlook of the legislator, steadily guiding his actions and structuring his voting? The answer is not altogether clear. An intensive study of state legislators in four states (California, New Jersey, Ohio, and Tennessee) identifies three fairly distinct role orientations: *"trustee"* (the legislator who sees himself as a free agent, bound only to follow his conscience and convictions), *"delegate"* (the legislator who senses a strong obligation to consult his constituents and to follow their instructions), and *"politico"* (the legislator who expresses both trustee and delegate role orientations). The study's findings conflict with the stereotype that most legislators see themselves as delegates of their constituencies. In none of the four states do more than 20 per cent of the legislators subscribe to the delegate role orientation. Conversely, at least 55 per cent of the legislators in each state hold the role orientation of trustee, and for Tennessee the figure is 81 per cent. The authors of *The Legislative System* suggest that the trustee role may have become a "functional necessity" for legislators because the work of government has become increasingly difficult for constituents to follow and understand.

A recent study of Pennsylvania legislators by Frank J. Sorauf reports conflicting findings. Fewer than one-third of the members are classified as "trustees." In this state the pre-eminent role assumed by legislators is that of delegate:

> The localism that ties a legislator to his constituents flourishes in Pennsylvania, more widely perhaps than in comparable states. "Servicing the constituents" absorbs an important part of every legislator's attention. The representative with pockets full of driver's license applications for his personal processing is not an uncommon sight in the General Assembly. Many legislative campaigns are fought on the issue of what the incumbent legislator did or did not "get" for the district in the two years of his stewardship. Every errand run in Harrisburg, every patronage job garnered for a constituent, every road paved or repaved in the district scores valuable points in the home town or county.

Relations between legislators and constituencies tend to elude labeling and firm generalization. The candidate who replaces the incumbent, for example, does not necessarily inherit his views toward representation. It is wholly conceivable that a legislator who attempts to represent every vagrant spark of constituency interest will be replaced by one who sees his role as trustee, or vice versa. There is individuality in politics, as well as in most everything else.

Yet in certain respects legislator-constituency relations can be said to follow general patterns, at least in northern legislatures. An assortment of studies, roughly parallel in approach, yields two main findings concerning linkages between legislators and their constituencies.

The first is that state legislators who are elected in districts atypical of their party are more likely to be party "mavericks," crossing lines to support positions held by the other party, than are those legislators who represent districts typical of their party. Party regulars are the products of constituencies with distinctive attributes: the typical Democratic state legislator is elected in an urban, low-income district; the typical Republican state legislator is elected in a rural district or an upper-income suburban or urban district. Democrats who are elected in districts with notable Republican characteristics (*e.g.*, rural) and Republicans who are elected in districts with notable Democratic characteristics (*e.g.*, low-income metropolitan) find loyalty to their respective party positions difficult to maintain. Constituency interests may well have first claim on their votes. The evidence is that party behavior has to be understood mainly, although not exclusively, in terms of constituency factors. To a remarkable extent the parties are what their *steadfast* constituencies make them.

The other salient finding is that the margin by which a candidate wins election tends to be associated with his subsequent voting behavior in the legislature. Legislators who are elected by close margins are more likely to be sensitive to constituency interests than are legislators who are elected by wide margins. Specifically, legislators from *competitive* districts (whose socio-economic characteristics ordinarily are mixed, neither distinctly Republican nor distinctly Democratic) tend to cross party lines more frequently than legislators from *noncompetitive* districts (whose socio-economic characteristics tend to be notably Democratic or notably Republican). Not surprisingly, members from noncompetitive districts have fewer anxieties over re-election and are generally the leading party loyalists in the legislature. Viewed in another light, competitive districts with mixed socio-economic characteristics tend to produce "moderate" legislators in both parties, while noncompetitive districts with dominant socio-economic characteristics tend to produce "liberal" Democrats and "conservative" Republicans.

Finally, in their role as representatives, legislators have a special concern in advancing the interests of the local and state party organizations to which they belong. They also have a vantage point excellently suited to reward the "machine" and its members. Influencing the allocation of patronage is a well known means for transmitting benefits to the party, and governors and bureaucrats hear a great deal from legislators about the need for jobs for deserving party members. Legislative investigations provide an opportunity for "out-party" legislators to come to the aid of their party. A vigorous investigation of an administrative agency, for example, may open the floodgates of public criticism, bringing embarrassment to the governor and his party.

The best means for advancing party interests is available in legislation itself. This is often a matter of exceptional simplicity for the party that controls both houses and the governorship—all that is necessary is to decide what is to be done and to fashion symbolic defenses for the action. The typical member does not create "party interest" legislation; he merely goes along with it. Where party control is divided between the houses or between governor and legislature, efforts in the interest of party usually take some form of harassment.

Legislation designed to serve broad public purposes can be used either to improve party fortunes or to embarrass the other party. One example would be the creation of new judgeships in districts in which the majority party is virtually certain to win while ignoring the need for judges in districts held by the other party. There are also opportunities in appropriations bills to place the governor on the spot, perhaps by making extravagant increases in public assistance payments or state employee salaries in order to invite an uncomfortable, unpopular veto. Redistricting legislation is, of course, a standing invitation to the majority party to construct districts that will improve its chances in elections and diminish those of the minority party. *Baker v. Carr* and *Reynolds v. Sims* have taken some of the slack out of redistricting decisions, but they have not eliminated gerrymandering in the interest of party or individual security.

Opportunities to press the party cause are limited only by failure of imagination. The legislature may decide to provide for minority party representation in city councils in major cities as a means of advancing local party interests. To indulge and attract city firemen and policemen, it may reduce their work weeks, provide various financial benefits for them (to be paid by the city), or hand them other levers to employ against their local governments. Or the legislature may dip into local administration itself by altering the powers of the mayor—his power over appointments, for example—or by transferring local functions from the city to the county in order to transfer control from one party to the other (so-called "ripper" legislation). In sum, "party interest" legislation is a recipe with two ingredients, each important. One part is ingenuity and the other is dissimulation. Opportunity and circumstance dictate which party puts the recipe together.

OVERSIGHT OF ADMINISTRATION

Surveillance or oversight of the administration has long been regarded as an essential function of representative assemblies. The grounds for surveillance can be stated simply. Legislatures adopt laws that create administrative agencies, and these in turn are assigned functions and responsibilities. The legislature establishes an agency and provides for its organization, for the hiring of personnel, and for the development of agency procedures. Bureaucrats are hired, governed, and removed under general or specific regulations stipulated by the legislature. With each session of the legislature new laws are passed that require administrative agencies to perform certain tasks established by the legislature. The legislature's decisions may require an agency to undertake new ventures or to modify or eliminate old ones. The legislature may decide to change statutory or administrative policy because, among other things, legislators have learned of hardships that have been imposed on the public, because interest groups contend that they are being seriously disadvantaged by existing policies, because administrators contend that an existing policy is not susceptible of effective administration, or because new conditions or information seem to argue for new policy.

The law of the legislature is steadily in flux. Just as no statute can settle a matter for all time, no language in a statute can guarantee that the policy will be administered as the legislature intended. If for no other reason, the legislature's self-interest demands that it oversee administration to learn whether agencies are complying with legislative intent.

Legislative oversight serves a variety of purposes: to keep the executive establishment responsive and accountable, to promote rationality and efficiency in the formulation and administration of public policy, to reap party advantage, and to advance the causes of individual legislators and interest groups.

Several methods are employed by the legislature in its attempt to make the executive behave. The legislature's lawmaking powers are used steadily to control administrative units. Legislation, as noted, can prescribe administrative functions, duties, and conduct. The consideration of administration bills affords legislative committees the chance to inquire into the work of agencies. Ordinarily, the best opportunity to review and influence administrative behavior occurs during the process of considering the governor's budget. At this point administrators can be asked to account for the performance of their agencies, to explain past expenditures, and to justify the funds requested for the new fiscal year. For reasons to be noted later, budget review by the legislature in many states is often more imposing in theory than in practice; nonetheless, bureaucrats have no reason to take the power lightly.

Although lawmaking provides the central method of legislative control over the executive branch, there are also other ways by which the legislature makes its influence felt. The selection of administrative personnel is usually a vital legislative interest. In a few states executive officials, such as the secretary of state or the treasurer, are elected by the legislature rather than by the people. Under this arrangement, legislative control over administration obviously is enhanced. Some measure of control over administrative personnel is achieved through the requirement that major appointments by the governor be confirmed by the senate (occasionally by a council or by the legislature as a whole). Intense bargaining frequently characterizes the appointment process. If confirmation requires a two-thirds vote, the minority party may have sufficient votes to wring concessions from the governor—patronage and policy are sometimes the price of confirmation. In a few states, the power of the governor to remove administrative officials is contingent upon legislative approval, ordinarily that of the senate. Finally, in all states except Oregon, the legislature possesses the power of impeachment. In practical terms, the impeachment power is of scant significance and is seldom used. It is scarcely more appropriate for legislative control of administration than is Russian roulette for assuaging boredom—both neglect, and possibly forfeit, intermediate applications.

Few matters of state government have more intrinsic interest for legislators than matters of personnel. For one thing, policy may be at stake—policy can be strengthened or imperiled by the men who administer it. More important, usually, is patronage. Where state merit systems are comprehensive, legislators may see the civil service as a vast wasteland. But when jobs can be made available for supporters, legislative interest runs high; access to patronage may prove to be a critical resource in the life of the legislator. Hence it is that oversight of hiring and firing practices may be motivated as much by the desire of legislators to bolster their own careers as to promote efficient, rational, or responsible administration.

Legislative control of administration sags in the absence of specific information concerning administrative programs and practices. In the ordinary course of considering legislation and appropriations, standing committees collect information—useful, if often random, in assaying the performance of administrative units. In addition, legislatures use investigating committees, various other interim or recess committees, and research agencies such as legislative councils, to collect and analyze information concerning the administration of state programs. Almost any aspect of state government may come under legislative examination, although investigations of correctional and educational institutions and of the major spending departments, such as highways and public welfare, seem to be especially common. It is difficult to generalize concerning the value of state investigating committees as instruments of legislative oversight. Some states make far more use of them than others. Performances are similarly uneven. Some investigating committees are no more than instruments to harass the governor or members of his administration. Some appear to be preoccupied with gaining and holding a public audience. Still others uncover abuses and maladministration, and focus public attention on conditions that call for corrective action. The possibility of legislative investigation doubtless contributes to administrative responsibility and rectitude.

That the legislature has both rationale and methods for influencing and supervising the administration does not mean that the function of oversight is conducted imaginatively or effectively. Undoubtedly the legislature makes its presence felt on occasion, although it seldom gets high marks for budget review, which is generally regarded as the crucial test of surveillance. Oversight tends to be episodic, partial, and selective. The legislature as a whole is not organized to struggle with the administration as a whole; but one committee can occasionally engage a particular agency, and even one legislator may be able to upset administrative equilibrium. The individual legislator engages in a form of oversight when he intercedes with agencies on behalf of constituents affected by administrative procedures or rulings; in his efforts to soften the impact of bureaucracy and to achieve redress of grievances the legislator ordinarily is highly successful. However modest "errand-running" may appear as a function of the legislator, it comes close to being the best illustration of continuing, effective oversight. It is similarly, of course, a function of representation. Very probably, legislative attempts to oversee the administration reach a high point when the legislature is controlled by one party and the administration is held by the other party. The motivations for oversight, in these circumstances, are usually rooted deep in party politics.

If legislative oversight is less effective in the states than it is in the United States Congress, which is undoubtedly the case, the reasons are not hard to find. The obstacles to oversight are monumental. The provision for biennial sessions is a major impediment. A legislature in session two or three months, or even six, out of twenty-four has scant time to devote to supervising the administration; the typical legislator takes the administration for granted until there are hints of a major scandal. The typical short session is also a deterrent to oversight. The presence of amateur legislators in great number, the shortage of staff aides, the press of other business, the contagion of sensational issues, the loyalty to party platoons, the lack of continuity in legislative membership—each of these factors contributes something to diminishing the legislators' concern and capacity to engage in steady, resourceful oversight of the administration. Oversight appears in bits and pieces. Among some legislators at least, the tendency is to search randomly for administrative weaknesses, and, having discovered something, to lash out. This does not contribute necessarily to effective oversight, but it may well disarm administrators and upset administrative activities *and* complacency. The value of these forays probably must be judged case by case.

Constitutional Limitations on the Legislature

Legislative creativity in the states, when and where it is found, exists despite the ideology and provisions of state constitutions. Without apparent exception, state constitutions in 1966 cast a net of suspicion over the legislature by circumscribing or limiting its powers and by making it difficult for state government to keep pace with the ideas and forms of mid-twentieth century America. Yet, in an earlier era, James W. Hurst has observed, legislatures occupied a strong place among governmental institutions:

> The early constitutions gave the legislature broad power. There they bore witness to its high public standing. The first state constitutions simply vested "legislative" power in described bodies. The grant implied the historic sweep of authority that Parliament had won, except as this was limited by vague implications to be drawn from the formal separation of powers among legislature, executive, and courts.

> Typically, the early constitution makers set no procedural requirements for the legislative process. They wrote a few declarations or limitations of substantive policy making. But these generally did no more than declare what contemporary opinion or community growth had already so deeply rooted as to require no constitutional sanction. . . .

What the public bestows on institutions it can take away. The first thing to be withdrawn from the early state legislatures, it seems, was popular confidence in the institution and in its members. This was the result of a train of scandals involving legislatures in the early and middle decades of the nineteenth century. The loss of standards of rectitude appeared in state after state—only the details differed. There were cases of extravagant spending and reckless borrowing, of the bribery of legislators, of the passage of special and local legislation in outrageous quantity, and of legislative collusion with private interests. The power of the legislature, so it must have appeared, was up for grabs.

But legislative corruption was only one theme in the story unfolded during this period. The other was the democratization of American society. As legislatures began to come under the control of the people, men of substance became wary. An unbridled legislature could upset established ways, imperiling property and the economic order. To those who were apprehensive over democracy itself there were good reasons for checking the power of the legislature. Corruption and fear of democracy, point and counterpoint, led to the legislature's undoing in the last half of the nineteenth century. Byron W. Abernethy writes:

> Between 1864 and 1880, thirty-five new constitutions were adopted in nineteen states. Distrust of the legislature was the predominant characteristic of all of them. Records of these conventions contain pages on pages of vigorous denunciation of state legislatures by the most outstanding members of the conventions. In the constitutions they drafted, they sought to prevent a recurrence of the evils they denounced, by incorporating not only new proscriptions on what the legislature might do, but also extensive legislation regulating and controlling the new economic interests to which earlier legislators had fallen victim. Hence these constitutions added provisions defining and regulating railroads, business practices, trusts, monopolies and interlocking directorates, corporations, the marketing and watering of corporate securities, and the regulation of banking and financial institutions. New prohibitions on the passing of local and special legislation were added. By 1880 the pattern for state constitutions as legal codes, and as obstructions to the free exercise of legislative power, was clearly set.

SPECIFIC LIMITATIONS

Today, the typical state constitution contains numerous provisions that curb legislative authority. Although there are obvious differences between the constitutions of the states, a general pattern of limitations may be detected. Included, frequently, are provisions that: (1) prohibit the legislature from enacting specific kinds of legislation; (2) impose detailed requirements concerning legislative procedure; (3) settle questions that ordinarily would be handled through legislation; and (4) establish the initiative and referendum, permitting voters to participate directly in lawmaking.

Legislation. Constitutional provisions that restrict the power of the legislature to legislate—the most significant band of limitations—are of several main types. All state constitutions contain a bill of rights, the main thrust of which is to deny the legislature the right to do certain things. These sections may not be limited to a listing of "inalienable" rights. For example, the bill of rights may prohibit lotteries (Georgia), establish the penalty for murder (Oregon), prohibit dueling and set a penalty for violation (Iowa), or regulate proceedings in eminent domain (Colorado). In addition, there are state constitutions in which the "rights" section contains provisions dealing with collective bargaining, other rights of labor, and discrimination by private employers. Such provisions necessarily constrict legislative discretion.

All but a few state constitutions carry proscriptions against the passage of special, private, or local legislation—that is, bills which deal with specific local governments, individuals, or corporations. Special legislation reached its zenith in the years after 1850. Legislators wrote law after law granting individuals relief (or exemptions) from the application of general laws, conferring astonishing advantages on private groups, and regulating local governments in extravagant detail. The logroll substituted for deliberation, and public policy of general significance became a shrinking segment of legislative output. Inevitably, such abuses quickened interest in reform. Hence, when the constitution makers of the latter part of the nineteenth century set about to draft new constitutions, they put together lengthy lists of subjects on which private or local legislation was prohibited. The legislature's law was to be of a general or public character. Although modern legislatures have discovered ways to circumvent the prohibitions concerning special legislation, they have much less leeway today than they had in 1850 or 1860.

Many complaints concerning constitutional limitations converge on the central issue of the legislature's power over state finances. By any standard, the limitations imposed on the legislature are harsh. The legislature's taxing power may be diminished by provisions that establish maximum tax rates, specify uniformity (one effect of which is to prohibit *graduated* income and other taxes), and set forth exemptions. The legislature's authority to incur debt is under similar constitutional control in nearly all states. A variety of limitations obtains, including those which limit borrowing to a certain amount, prohibit the legislature from extending its credit to other persons or agencies or from incurring debt, or require a popular referendum to approve state borrowing. These restrictions are generally viewed as unrealistic, as hindrances to effective state government, and as shields behind which timorous, irresolute legislators may hide. Plainly, they impair legislative autonomy and integrity.

But the erosion of legislative fiscal powers has not been confined to the curbs on the taxing power and debt incurment. A further loss has resulted from the earmarking of funds. Under this arrangement, developed in part to evade constitutional debt limitations, states have established an unusual assortment of special funds to finance specific governmental activities, such as those in the areas of public education, highways, fish and game conservation, and old age pensions. Revenues collected from particular taxes are earmarked for particular purposes or departments—*e.g.*, revenues from gasoline and motor vehicle taxes are assigned to the construction and maintenance of highways while revenues from fishing and hunting licenses are devoted to fish and game management. In thirty states, according to a 1965 report of the Tax Foundation, continuing or earmarked appropriations constitute one-half or more of total expenditures; in some the proportion may reach as high as 90 per cent, thereby giving the legislature control over a mere 10 per cent of the total budget. Some states have more than 100 special funds, some of which are established by constitutional mandate and others by statute. Where earmarking is extensive, the power of the legislature over the state budget is in many respects perfunctory. The state itself is hamstrung—its most urgent needs cannot be satisfied by funds already frozen for other purposes. Even surpluses may not be used for general state requirements. Lobbies whose programs are supported by earmarked funds rank among the most zealous guardians found anywhere in and around the legislature.

Procedures. Legislative procedures are not matters which lie solely within the jurisdiction of the legislature. On the contrary, many constitutions establish basic procedural requirements to be followed in the lawmaking process. For example, a constitution may specify that the legislature must keep a journal, that each bill be given a title, that each bill be limited to a single subject, that each bill be given a reading in full, or that each bill be given three readings on separate days. It may stipulate that a certain number of members can insist on a roll call and that a roll-call vote must be held on final passage of each bill. Numerous other similar requirements have found their way into the constitutions. Even though the technical elements of the legislative process are regulated in sharp detail, there is no assurance that the legislature will strictly observe the requirements. Many of the provisions earn no more than a wink. Yet, failure to follow these provisions in full (for example, confining each bill to a single subject) may lead to court tests of the validity of statutes. Students of legislation believe that most legislative procedure requirements could be stricken from constitutions without impairing the legislative process in the slightest.

Statutory Law in the Constitution. Constitutions which contain quantities of "statutory" law may also be said to limit the powers of the legislature. The length, rigidity, and complexity of state constitutions have largely resulted from the inclusion of vast amounts of law that should have been adopted as general legislation, easily subject to revision by the legislature of the day. The constitution is an exception which fails to include multiple provisions that regulate corporate enterprise, monopolies and trusts, details of the judicial process, taxation and contract procedures, local school board organization and administration, state administrative organization and administration, municipal corporations, or even labor-management relations and conditions of work. Many of these provisions are not especially pertinent to current American society, and some are serious obstacles to rational decision making. In one sense, they testify to the credulity of nineteenth century constitution-makers who were set, in this as in other matters, to curb legislative excesses and ended by draining the institution of its vitality.

Initiative and Referendum. Finally, state constitutions place an indirect limitation on legislative authority when they invite direct citizen participation in the lawmaking process. Slightly more than one-third of the states have adopted provisions for the initiative and referendum. The initiative permits a certain number of voters to propose a law for inclusion on the ballot in the coming election. Through this means, voters may enact laws which have been blocked in the legislature. The referendum also allows for popular invasion of the legislative task. Sometimes called the "popular veto," it provides that certain legislative and constitutional enactments must receive popular approval before taking effect. State borrowing, tax levies, and liquor regulations are frequent subjects of referendum legislation. Under the "protest" referendum, voters who are opposed to a measure adopted by the legislature can demand that it be submitted for popular approval; ordinarily a majority vote is required for adoption.

In practice, the initiative and referendum may not be so much the instruments of an involved citizenry as those of political interest groups impatient with customary lawmaking because they have been unable to extract favorable settlements from it. Of course, there are many good arguments on behalf of these devices of direct legislation. Yet, whatever the experience with the initiative and referendum, the fact remains that their use collides with the notion of placing responsibility for legislation upon the legislature.

Other Limitations. To complete the brief sketch of constitutional limitations on the legislature, it is necessary to direct attention to the legislature's position vis-à-vis the national government and vis-à-vis the courts. State legislative authority, viewed broadly, is *residual*; that is, it includes all powers not awarded by the national constitution to national agencies or not awarded by the state constitution to other state or local agencies. Although this residual authority results in a substantial band of powers being left to the legislatures, there are also accompanying restrictions. The national constitution limits the states, and thus their legislatures, in ways familiar to every schoolboy: it prohibits states from coining money, negotiating treaties, adopting bills of attainder or ex post facto laws, and so on. Moreover, Supreme Court decisions have served to "expand" the Bill of Rights by giving the citizen protection against state and local governments in the same way that protection is afforded against the national government. Finally, the doctrine of *implied limita-tions,* imposed by some *state* courts, holds that the legislature is limited to those powers specifically enumerated in the state constitution. Hence, constitutions which list specific legislative powers may ultimately deny the legislature's general or plenary powers. Relief from court rulings on "implied limitations" can be sought only in constitutional amendments to enlarge legislative authority.

At one time severe constitutional limitations on the legislature seemed to hold the definitive answer to legislative waywardness. Today, students of politics are more likely to argue that such limitations are the result of illusion, misapprehension, and bias. The illusion is that "solutions" wrought in one era will suffice in the next; the misapprehension is that constitutions are appropriate instruments for the settlement of contro-versies over public policy; the bias is that legislative judgment is not to be trusted, especially in matters of money.

Political-environmental Limitations on the Legislature

To the string of constitutional provisions that limit the legisla-ture, we should add other factors of a "political-environmental" character. For convenience, these may be placed in the following categories: (1) widespread discontent over the legislature; (2) growth of the governor's legislative role; (3) obstacles to leadership by the legislature; and (4) growth of federal power.

DISCONTENT OVER THE LEGISLATURE

Popular discontent over the performance of American state legislatures is not new. It was public uneasiness concerning the legislature in the period after 1850 that led to a wave of constitutional revisions to limit legislative powers. Legislators themselves testify readily to the lamentable image of state assemblies. Although it is difficult to gauge the effect of the public's lack of confidence in the legislature, it is reasonable to sur-mise that a political institution short on public esteem loses influence in the political system. Political institutions, no less than political men, have need of high public standing. Prestige (or "standing") is a political resource, convertible into political influence, in much the same way that votes, wealth, or education are political resources for political men. The legislature's resources in public standing, it appears, are exceedingly thin. The effect of this is to weaken its position in the bargaining systems that dominate state politics.

State legislatures are indicted on a number of counts. The charges range from the quality of the legislature as an institution to the quality of the men and women who hold legislative office. Critics do not agree on what is wrong with state assemblies, but only that something is wrong. If all the specific complaints made by persons impatient with state legislatures were set down, the list might easily stretch beyond the length suitable here. Legislatures attract discontent simply by being legislatures. To avoid a profusion of themes, this essay lodges the criticisms within four broad categories.

Unrepresentativeness and Minority Rule. For at least the last two decades, no feature of state politics has received more criticism than systems of legislative representation. Endless statistics have been assembled to show that virtually all legislatures have had apportionment systems tilted to give rural areas more representation than warranted by their populations. Problems posed by the devaluation of the urban dweller's vote have been especially acute in those states in which city governments lack "home rule" powers. As of 1960, the doctrine of representation according to population had become so shorn of meaning that the vote of a resident of a large city was worth less than half of a vote of a resident of a rural area. Bent on preserving their privileges, rural and small-town leaders of the legislatures either ignored constitutional obligations to redistrict following each census or else allocated representatives on the basis of formulas which undervalued population. Constitutional provisions on apportionment helped to make their defense of rural power surprisingly easy. Not so easy, however, was the task of defending legislative prestige in the face of massive evidence of unrepresentativeness.

As a result of a series of Supreme Court decisions in the early 1960s, which upset legislative and congressional apportionment systems, the picture changed markedly. Under the press of the equal-population doctrine adopted by the Court, state legislators trudged back to their drawing boards to sketch new district lines, awarding urban and suburban areas significantly more representation. Rural power was cut back. Prospects for "majority rule" were improved. How the new and weightier representation of the cities may affect the legislatures' performances and the critics' valuations remains to be seen. In the "conventional wisdom" of political analysts, malapportionment often has been treated as the main obstacle to revitalization of the legislatures. The validity of this proposition will now become testable—in perhaps a decade. All that is certain for the moment, however, is that urban and suburban legislators (and the interests they represent) will have more influence in the legislative process than they had in the past.

Corruption and Conflict-of-Interest. It is a fair guess that no stories about the legislature are more likely to dampen public confidence in the institution or to move some citizens into the queues of reformers than those which touch on the ethical standards of legislators. Easily made, the charge of corruption among legislators is never easy to document. In some states, the issue is always near the surface, kept there at times by the accusations of legislators. For example, an article published in 1964 by Paul Simon, a well known state senator in Illinois, carries an estimation that "one-third of the members accept payoffs":

Most of these are recorded as legal fees, public-relations services, or "campaign contributions," though a campaign may be months away. If questioned, the recipient simply denies that the payment had anything to do with legislative activity. This makes it technically legal. A somewhat smaller number of payoffs are not veiled at all; cold cash passes directly from one hand to the other. . . . A few legislators go so far as to introduce some bills that are deliberately designed to shake down groups which oppose them and which pay to have them withdrawn. These bills are called "fetchers," and once their sponsors develop a lucrative field, they guard it jealously.

Another account by Duane Lockard is not vastly different:

Rhode Island's race tracks are the ultimate source of much of the corruption in the state. Tieups between legislators who receive special favors from race-track operators are frequently reported in the press, but to show associations which arouse suspicion and to prove that a legislator was "bought" are two different matters. The majority leader of the House . . . has for many years been an attorney for one of the race tracks. One cannot conclude from this fact alone that the actions of the majority leader on race-track issues are influenced thereby, but at the very least there would seem to be a serious conflict of interests. Similarly, many legislators have been in the employ of the race tracks in such jobs as clerk at a betting window. Often it has been shown that these legislators and other paid staff members of the legislature were recorded as "present" in the House of Representatives while in fact they were working at the tracks.

To accusations that bribery, extortion, peculation, and collusion generally dominate the actions of state legislatures, one must demur. There is ample testimony that many legislatures are rarely tainted either by allegations or instances of venality. "Fetcher" or "Mae West" bills ("Come up and see me sometime!") doubtless appear in some states, perhaps even with frequency, but there is no evidence to suggest that they are common in legislatures throughout the country. Not the least, and not the only, reason for this is that bribery in any form is technically a difficult problem—the larger the number of individuals recruited for or privy to the cabal, the greater the chances of exposure.

Conflict-of-interest is much more common than corruption. It, too, has contributed something to the obloquy that has settled over the legislature. Conflict-of-interest for the legislator arises when he uses his public office to secure private gain, either for himself or for his associates. The boundaries of conflict-of-interest are not always easy to see. But the legislator who is a lawyer, a stockholder in a race track, an owner of a finance company, a contractor, a real estate or liquor store operator, or an insurance man, to pick a few examples, can hardly fail to detect the conflict-of-interest problem when legislation affecting his private welfare is under consideration. Like Congress, state legislatures have not rushed to adopt codes of ethics that prohibit certain activities on the part of members (*e.g.*, appearing before state agencies on a contingent-fee basis, selling goods or services to state agencies, and so on), require members to file a record of their financial interests in enterprises under the jurisdiction of state agencies, and illuminate the points at which conflicts between public and private roles are likely to arise.

Trivia Plus Bizarre Behavior. State legislatures come under review regularly for failing to use time and talent prudently. One charge is that the typical legislature begins work slowly, working a two- or three-day week for the first couple of months or more, and ends work in a frenzy, meeting in round-the-clock sessions. And the subjects of deliberation, it is pointed out, are not always of monumental significance. Editorials point to the fact that the legislature identified the starling as a dirty bird and called for its extinction, that it rejected a bill to permit the use of slingshots in frog hunts, or that it considered changing the official state bird from the cardinal to the purple martin. There is a succession of accounts suggesting that legislators never quite come to terms with their task:

> The Ohio Legislature, after nine weeks of sessions, is just limping along weakly, almost aimlessly. . . . Hearings drone on. . . . The bills debated daily during sessions are what the legislators themselves call "cats and dogs," unimportant bills. (*Cleveland Press,* March 18, 1965.)

> The Minnesota Legislature adjourns on a limp note. Often there has been, at two-year intervals, the temptation to say that a particular session is the worst in history. That probably is an untrue designation of the 1965 affair, yet legislators must share with citizens the let-down feeling of a lack of notable accomplishment. (*The Minneapolis Tribune,* May 24, 1965.)

> It has been a lazy legislature [California]. It took long weekends in the first part of the session and got behind, it passed out of committee nonsense bills that should have been killed, and it expended the greater part of its not unlimited intellectual energies in the free-hand drawing of senatorial lines that very possibly will not meet the "one person, one vote" test. (*The San Francisco Chronicle,* June 18, 1965.)

The notoriety sometimes attaching to the legislature may also be the result of the occasional antics of members. One account, this of the Texas legislature, will have to suffice. Willie Morris writes:

> One night, in a bitter floor debate in the lower house, one legislator pulled the cord out of the amplifier system, another hit him from the blindside with a tackle; there was mass pushing, hitting, clawing, and exchanges about one another's wives, mistresses, and forebears. Sweethearts and wives, who were allowed on the floor with friends and secretaries cowered near the desks. In the middle of the brawl, a barbershop quartet of legislators quickly formed at the front of the chamber and, like a dance band during a saloon fight, sang "I Had a Dream, Dear."

Failure of Party Responsibility. According to many political scientists, the major deficiency of the American state legislature is its irresponsibility, a condition that results from the weakness and lack of unity of legislative parties. Weak parties leave the public unable to hold any group firmly accountable for the record of the legislature, for what it does or fails to do. Advocates of "party responsibility" have in mind a party system with two vigorous parties, each competing with the other, making their cases to the voters of the state in terms of programs and policies. The party winning control of the government is committed to translate its campaign platform and pledges into public policy. The next election, in turn, enables voters to judge the party's performance in office and to estimate which party will best serve their purposes over the next two or four years. The key idea in the party responsibility model is the responsibility of the majority party to the voters. The aim is to take some of the mystery out of legislative politics by fastening the responsibility for legislative decisions on the party group.

For a variety of reasons the responsibility model is approximated in only a few states. In one-party states, for example, party is no more than an umbrella under which anyone can stand; factions pass for parties but factional responsibility is difficult to identify. In a great many two-party states, malapportionment, staggered terms of office, and other factors make it unlikely that one of the major parties can capture the governorship and both houses at the *same* time, a minimum requirement for responsibility. Furthermore, even in competitive states, many legislative districts are so thoroughly dominated by one party that voters seldom have a meaningful choice. Finally, legislative party responsibility frequently founders on the shoals of localism. Critics contend that responsible legislative performance is all but impossible when legislative parties are weak and ineffective. The legislature's business tends to be lost on a public wholly unable to fit the thousands of individual legislative decisions into categories conspicuous enough to be seen and evaluated.

Complaints against the legislature are familiar facts of daily civics. *Ironically, whether the indictments are accurate may be much less important than that many people are prepared to accept them.* A little evidence goes a long way. Each specific example of waywardness, it seems, contributes to the massive generalization that describes the legislature as an institution in decline. In the argot of popular appraisal, a bill to raise legislative salaries is a "salary grab," a vote to block an appointment by the governor is "callous partisanship," a failure to accept the governor's program is "obstructionist," a move to strengthen rule by the majority party is "the most coldly cynical performance seen in years." It is hard to shake the impression that when the legislature goes along with the governor its actions will be viewed as "rubber stamp," and when it asserts itself its behavior will be viewed as "obstructionist." The legislature occupies an unhappy position among American political institutions. Part of the reason for this is that the legislature is not only what it makes of itself but what conventional interpretation makes of it.

GROWTH OF GOVERNOR'S ROLE AS LEGISLATOR

Under the first state constitutions, supreme power rested with state legislatures. The powers of state governors, by contrast, were sharply circumscribed. In the usual arrangement, the governor was appointed by the legislature for a short term, perhaps of one year. He was not expected to recommend legislation to the assembly, and in only two states did he possess the veto power. Other executive officials were elected independently of the governor, further diminishing his authority. A broad sketch of this period would show the governors weak in power, weak in public esteem, and everywhere under the thumb of the legislature. But institutions change. Today, the positions of the legislature and the governor are almost completely reversed; devices for containment once applied to the governor now apply to the legislature. Leadership of the legislature has become not so much a legislative as a gubernatorial function. Constitutions, statutes, conventions, and popular expectations testify in state after state that the governor is, as the saying goes, the "chief legislator."

A number of circumstances and powers are linked to the emergence and development of the governor as a legislative leader. The governor's pre-eminence in state politics came more from an accretion of influence than from wresting leadership from the legislature. At one point in the nineteenth century, following the decline of the legislature, both legislative and executive branches could be fairly described as weak. As powers once again were assembled, however, they were assigned or came to rest with the governor. Although there are notable differences among the states in the powers assigned to the governor, according to a study by Joseph A. Schlesinger, his general legal-constitutional position is strong in most parts of the country outside of the South. State constitutions empower the governor to recommend measures to the legislature; his messages, given at the opening of sessions and also at intervals, ordinarily establish the main outlines of the legislative agenda. Specific proposals introduced by the governor's main supporters in the legislature fill in the framework; in most cases, these bills will have been drafted in administrative agencies and cleared through the governor's office. "Administration bills" are the principal bills of almost any session of almost any legislature. They pre-empt the legislators' time and tend to become the chief standard by which sessions are evaluated.

A second constitutional power of the governor enables him to call special sessions of the legislature; not only is he authorized to bring the legislators back to the capital but he determines (in the great majority of states) what subjects will be brought before them for consideration.

And it is not unusual during a regular session for occasional hints to be conveyed that a special session will be called if the legislature fails to act on one of his major bills. The special session, in a word, is usually the "governor's" session, called as a result of his initiative and influenced by his preferences.

The major constitutional power of the governor is the veto, authorized in every state except North Carolina. Four out of every five governors have, in addition, an item veto on appropriations bills. Well over a majority of the states specify that a two-thirds vote of both houses is needed to override the governor's veto. In the conflicts generated between governor and legislature as a result of vetoes, the governor plainly has the upper hand. Efforts to override a veto are nearly always unsuccessful in states such as Alabama, Illinois, Iowa, Michigan, New York, and Pennsylvania. Elsewhere, with a few exceptions, the legislatures' prospects of prevailing are not much better. Still, this is less than the whole story. The governor can also expect to win if he threatens the use of the veto; a threat is likely to induce legislative sponsors to rewrite a bill to meet his objections or even to abandon it. Cases also arise in which the legislature recalls from the governor a bill already passed because of word of an impending veto; a new version, the legislature reasons, may have a better chance. Finally, a few states have provisions for "executive amendment" under which the governor may return a bill to the legislature with recommendations for changes which would make it acceptable to him.

A distinctive source of the governor's ability to lead the legislature is in his authority over budget making. This responsibility is given the governor in forty-four states; in five other states it is vested in a board composed either of members of the executive branch or of members of both the executive and the legislative branches. Arkansas is the only state in which budget preparation is assigned to a legislative agency (the Legislative Council). The governor's ability to protect his budget is frequently related to constitutional allocations of power. The item veto, for example, is an important power, since it enables the governor to eliminate specific appropriations added to his budget by the legislature. Some state constitutions empower the governor to reduce appropriations for individual items. Limitations on the legislature similarly serve executive purposes. One example is the constitutional provision which specifically prohibits the legislature from increasing the governor's budget bill. Some states operate under procedures that award budget legislation priority in consideration. The main thrust of state constitutions, in this matter as in others, is to confer advantages on the governor and to place restrictions on the legislature.

Although the governor in "executive budget" states plays a critical role in shaping the state's fiscal and program policies, his powers are nevertheless limited in certain important respects. "Earmarking" of funds limits his choices as fully as it does the legislature's. The budget requests of departments administered by officials independently elected ordinarily do not come under central review. There also may be specific mandatory programs for which state finances are committed at a certain level, thus diminishing the governor's discretion. Finally, of course, the budget must be submitted to the legislature for its evaluation, modification, or acceptance.

In practice, legislative review of the budget is an uncertain element of the budget process. The difficulties that confront the legislature in budget review are enormous. The typical legislator is an amateur and the typical legislative session is brief. The data that support budget estimates are as complicated as they are elusive. A variety of policy questions, large and small, compete for the member's attention. Legislative staff assistance is often in short supply. One indication of the dilemma is that a fiscal review staff directly responsible to the legislature, such as a legislative council, is available in only about half the states. Lacking adequate resources for budget review, the legislature is dependent on the expertise of its members or on the advice and guidance of *executive* officials. At times, legislators depend on the counsel of interest groups. Despite the need for legislative post audits, legislative control over state finances may end once the appropriations bills have been passed. Arlene T. Shadoan contends:

> Too often legislative review of the budget is cursory, haphazard, and uninformed. The growth and the increase in complexity of the state's activities have made careful and informed review difficult, especially in view of the short period that the legislator has for budget consideration and the fact that legislation is, for most legislators, a second, if not secondary, occupation.

The fact that the governor carries the main responsibility for budget making does not mean that his budget will move through the legislature unscathed. Under certain circumstances—*e.g.,* control of one or both houses by the opposition party—cuts or additions are likely to be made. Protracted deadlock is not uncommon. Occasionally the governor runs into trouble with members of his own party who are bent on increasing (or less commonly, decreasing) appropriations. When the governor and the majority in the legislature are of the same party, in two-party states, the governor usually can expect strong support from his party and strong opposition from the minority party. In these states the budget frequently turns into a series of party issues. The governor does not invariably get his way on fiscal matters in any state. At times, his main opponents are lodged within the executive branch. The completed budget is a mixture of "gains" and "setbacks." Although the governor loses on some things, he wins far more often, and his victories are generally of wide-ranging significance. The budget adopted, it is worth remembering, ultimately determines what state government is all about.

The legislature's loss of parity with the governor may be identified as the outstanding fact of twentieth century state politics. The governor's ascendancy is attributable at least as much, and probably far more, to his role as state political leader as it is to legal-constitutional arrangements designed to strengthen the governorship or to limit the legislature. To borrow and bend a line from Richard Neustadt's analysis of the presidency, no legislator sits where the governor sits or sees what the governor sees. No legislator feels the pressures he feels or carries the responsibilities he carries. No legislator can claim to represent the state as a whole. If a state has a tradition of executive leadership and if the governor is disposed to lead, the resources with which to lead are at hand.

The governor's role as political leader is fashioned out of countless opportunities. While individual legislators strain for occasional newspaper coverage, the governor stands knee deep in correspondents. The massed drums of public relations and the steady fare of newspaper, radio, and television commentary make the governor the visible sign of state government and of state power. Crisis dramatizes the governor's responsibilities. The governor alone can focus sharp attention on state issues. Both the legislators and the public expect him to present a legislative program and to marshal support for it. To an important extent, at least in two-party states, the party stands for what he stands. He can center attention on legislators, put them on the hook or take them off. He can promote friends and frustrate rivals, advance or sandbag careers. Often he controls the legislature by controlling the route that leads to legislative power—commonly he influences the selection of the speaker, majority leaders, and important committee chairmen. The chances are one out of two that he knows the legislative process because he was a former legislator. If he uses patronage skilfully, he can promote his legislation and undermine bills he opposes; in some states he still has a massive supply of patronage. He can sometimes use state contracts in his bargaining for legislative votes. He is in a better position to logroll with legislators than they are with themselves; he can add momentum to the pet bills of individual legislators, or those of legislative blocs, in return for their support of administration bills. The fortunes of many legislators are linked to those of the governor's—if he wins, they win; if he loses, they lose.

In sum, superior visibility, superior constitutional position, superior staff assistance, superior claim to representation of statewide interests, superior position in the state party organization, and superior access to political resources (jobs, publicity, credit, wealth, prestige, information, etc.) give the governor the opportunity to make his office about what he chooses. Some governors elect not to exploit their advantages and some are rebuffed when they try. Furthermore, some governors must contend with rivals in the executive branch who have independent bases of support in the legislature. Much legislation is simply of no interest to the governor or to his administration, although legislators (or interest groups) may view it as important, even critical; legislators are often concerned about liquor and vehicle codes, local government organization, annexation law, and the regulation of opticians, but governors ordinarily are not. Some states have a tradition of the passive governor. Nonetheless, the general pattern in the states is one of gubernatorial leadership. When and where the legislature is ascendant, the explanation is usually that the governor has a deficiency in political resources or has opted for an "administrative" rather than a "policy-making" role. Like legislators, governors can choose to be spectators.

OBSTACLES TO LEADERSHIP BY THE LEGISLATURE

There are a number of reasons why legislatures are not suited to offer continuing leadership in state politics. First, it is rarely possible for the legislature to speak with a single, distinct voice. All legislators, as it were, play a role in explaining what the legislature has done or is about to do; the result, frequently, is a babble of conflicting voices. Moreover, there are always others outside the legislature who purport to speak for the members—not the least of these are major state and local party leaders who interpret legislative events in party language, adding to the dissonance of legislative discussion. Second, the multiple points of decision making cause legislative happenings to lack focus and articulation; critical actions occur at unexpected times and in out-of-the-way places. Third, legislative rules and procedures are cumbersome and complex, and may seem designed to help members elude responsibility for their decisions. The inability of the public to understand the legislature's processes does not necessarily breed distrust, but it seems likely to stifle interest. Fourth, no legislator or group of legislators can command press or radio attention in extent sufficient to rival that steadily given the governor. Fifth, the legislature has not been able to match the executive in gathering and processing information critical to the function of policy making.

Sixth, leadership is associated with the power to initiate; today's legislature is better equipped to review proposals than to generate them, to amend rather than to fashion. Legislators who perceive themselves as "inventors" (the initiators or creators of public policy) are found much less frequently than those who seem to be "ritualists" (the specialists in parliamentary procedure and in the mechanics of the legislator's job) or "tribunes" (the advocates and guardians of the people's interests). Seventh, government by committee is not conducive to leadership. Committees can inquire into government and can review, revise, and vote down legislation, but they do not frequently take the lead, establishing new directions by creating legislation.

Eighth, it is difficult to center leadership in an institution heavily populated by amateurs; in some states well over one-third of the legislators in any session will be freshman members. Low salaries, high turnover, infrequent meetings, and short sessions undermine efforts to professionalize legislative service. Ninth, legislative initiative often seems to be most apparent when legislation of narrow interest to the members or to the parties is under consideration—involving, for example, civil service, reapportionment, election law, and local political systems. Party-interest legislation is not likely to win the acclaim of the general public. Tenth, legislative politics weighs heavily on potential leaders, as suggested in this analysis by Coleman B. Ransone:

> [It] seems to be the nature of legislatures to cut down any aspiring single legislator who tries to assert leadership. When such a legislator occasionally does arise he is suspected, perhaps with good cause, to have designs on the governorship and hence is rejected as overly ambitious by his fellow legislators. He may be suspected also of the same ambitions by the incumbent governor who may assist in blocking the legislator's proposals.

Finally, both legislative and executive power are checked under conditions of "divided government"—that is, when one party controls the governor's office and the other party controls one or both houses of the legislature. Theoretically, the party helps to bridge the chasm separating the executive and the legislature. If the governor and both houses are controlled by the same party, the prospects are better that tensions between the two branches can be kept down and that the powers of each can be assembled for common purposes. Table 1, updating the original

Table 1: Elections in 32 States, 1930-50, and in 37 States, 1952-62, Showing Relation of Governor to Legislature in Terms of Party Control. *

Relation between Governor and Legislature	1930-50 (32 States) Number	Per Cent	1952-62 (37 States) Number	Per Cent
Governor Opposed	126	35.7	89	42.4
Governor Unopposed	227	64.3	121	57.6
Total Elections	353	100.0	210	100.0

* For the period 1930-50, fourteen states are excluded because one party continuously held the governorship and both houses of the legislature. These one-party states, mainly Democratic, were Alabama, Arkansas, Florida, Georgia, Louisiana, Mississippi, New Hampshire, North Carolina, Oklahoma, South Carolina, Tennessee, Texas, Virginia, and Vermont. During the period 1952-62, New Hampshire, Oklahoma, and Vermont entered the ranks of "competitive" states. Minnesota and Nebraska are excluded because they have nonpartisan legislatures. Alaska's tabulations begin with 1958 and Hawaii's with 1959.

Source: (1930-50) V. O. Key, Jr., and Corinne Silverman, "Party and Separation of Powers: A Panorama of Practice in the States," in *Public Policy*, eds. Carl J. Friedrich and J. Kenneth Galbraith. Cambridge: Harvard University, Graduate School of Public Administration, 1954, Table 3, p. 389.

work of V. O. Key, Jr. and Corinne Silverman, shows the incidence of divided government in *competitive* states during two intervals, 1930-50 and 1952-62. The extent of divided party control, substantial during the period 1930-50, was even greater during the period 1952-62. Over the latter interval, the chances were better than four out of ten that each new state election would leave the governor opposed by a majority of the opposite party in at least one of the two houses. Democratic governors were visited by this problem much more often than Republican governors. Division of control occurred most frequently in Nevada (entire period), Michigan, Montana, New Jersey, Arizona, and Connecticut.

A number of factors contribute to the disparities between party gubernatorial and legislative victories. Legislative malapportionment is one explanation for divided control. Other factors are the election of the legislature and executive for nonconcurrent terms, the existence of staggered elections for upper and lower houses, and the separation of gubernatorial and presidential elections. There are some grounds for believing that voters deliberately split party control between the branches. Whatever the reasons, divided government tends to promote conflict between the branches and to make it difficult to fix responsibility for decisions on either party. Under these circumstances, legislative power may degenerate into legislative assertiveness. Majority control of one or both houses will not permit the party that lacks the governorship to rule, but it will give the party endless opportunities to harass and obstruct the administration. There is no reason to believe that divided government either sparks legislative creativity or promotes effective government. Rather, it seems far more likely to lead to frustration, deadlock, irresponsibility, and party maneuvering in the interest of party "machines."

GROWTH OF FEDERAL POWER

To some extent the growth of the federal government's role in American life has proved inimical to the maintenance of the authority and autonomy of state legislatures. Under the impact of the Great Depression, World War II, the Cold War, and the revolutions in civil rights and in urban expectations, federal-state relations have changed markedly. Three developments are especially noteworthy. The first is the extraordinary expansion of federal responsibilities in fields previously dominated by states and localities. Although state legislatures can of course refuse to participate in federal aid programs, the practical necessity of paying for state services all but rules out this option. Moreover, the availability of federal monies permits state legislatures to meet popular demands for services without having to raise all the funds through state taxes. Not surprisingly, the inducement to participate transcends the legislature's desire to be master of its own house.

The second major development, closely related to the first, is the sharp increase in direct relations between the federal government and the cities. Many factors help account for this development, which leads to bypassing of state legislatures, but the most important seems to be that cities turn to the federal government for assistance when they find the legislatures unresponsive. Among the federal government's programs to aid today's cities are urban renewal, slum clearance, public housing, airport construction, air pollution control, urban mass transportation, and metropolitan planning. As these programs have grown, cities have edged away from the jurisdiction of state legislatures.

Finally, state legislatures everywhere have felt the powers of Congress and the decisions of the Supreme Court. Major laws of Congress—*e.g.*, the 1965 voting rights act—almost invariably intrude on the powers of state legislatures. Moreover, acts of Congress, together with Supreme Court rulings, have led to the pre-emption of certain fields of legislation, thereby diminishing the range of policy making open to state legislatures. The Supreme Court has invalidated state laws under three conditions: (1) when Congress has recorded its intention to pre-empt or occupy a particular field of legislation; (2) when state legislative enactments are judged in conflict with federal laws; and (3), of greatest controversy, when congressional pre-emption of a field of legislation can be inferred (*i.e.*, "pre-emption by implication"). State statutes dealing with subversion, for example, have fallen under the doctrine of federal legislative pre-emption. States' rights advocates in Congress have frequently introduced anti-pre-emption bills to offset Court rulings; on two occasions since 1955 an anti-pre-emption bill has passed the House of Representatives, only to be defeated in the Senate. In certain fields, state legislative power has been notably limited by the pre-emption doctrine.

State legislative power has been particularly affected by the Supreme Court's historic decision on racial desegregation in the public schools in 1954 and by its several decisions on legislative and congressional reapportionment in the early 1960s. It would be difficult to find better examples of national power than the reapportionment cases. It can fairly be said that the Supreme Court in the early 1960s contributed at least as much as governors, political interest groups, or political parties to shaping the agendas of state legislatures. Scarcely any legislature was able to escape the press of reapportionment business forced by the Court's decisions. No legislation seemed to receive greater priority than redistricting bills, and in some states entire sessions were dominated by struggles over district lines. Responding to social and economic problems largely ignored by the states, the President, Congress, and the Court have steadily eroded state power since the 1930s. The failure of legislative initiative in the states must be ranked among the principal reasons for the expansion of federal power and the redefinition of federal responsibilities.

Legislators and Legislative Tasks

The image of the state legislator as a person of high motivation, talent, and ambition to excel is scarcely ever conveyed in the popular mass media or academic literature. Such ingenuity or skills as he may possess, according to this typical casting, tend to be used for base private purposes, to promote narrow partisan causes, or to advance nonlegislative careers. To those who help mold public tastes and opinions, the legislator is not a man who brings skills to lawmaking tasks or treats his job seriously, but rather one adept at creating beguiling issues and at dodging authentic ones—a man good at going through public motions.

Legislators and the public, insiders and outsiders, ordinarily do not see the legislative institution in the same way. There is a persistent public belief, as noted earlier, that legislators fail to engage themselves seriously in the important tasks of the legislature, preferring instead to devote their energies to less worthy functions and activities—running errands for constituents, celebrating the legislature before visiting school children or local civic groups, harassing the governor, and dealing in patronage and local and state political problems, among other things. Our purpose here is not to try to weigh the accuracy of the general indictment but to suggest reasons why the over-all performance of the legislature may not be of critical importance to some, perhaps to many, legislators. The public's priorities and the legislator's priorities may be most notable for the degree to which they differ.

Two broad and tentative explanations may help to interpret the legislative condition. One centers on the legislator as he relates to his office. The other tries to explain the legislator's outlook as a "function" of the multiple environments in which he acts. Neither, of course, argues that state lawmakers fail to live up to expectations, neglecting or demeaning the critical tasks of the legislature, because they are perverse men (*e.g.*, willful partisans or obstructionists) although popular reporting sometimes carries more than a tinge of this suggestion.

THE LEGISLATOR AND HIS OFFICE

The effective and responsible lawmaker is endowed with qualities and attitudes not easily defined with precision. For one thing, what appears as "effective" or "responsible" behavior to one person may appear much less than this to another. The legislator who loyally represents his district, for example, might be judged "irresponsible" by observers who believe that statewide party programs ought to be accorded priority over constituency interests. And there are other obvious difficulties in judging these elusive qualities. Yet, in a more general sense, there may be wide agreement on the qualities of superior legislators. Presumably, there would be marked agreement on the need for legislators who are intelligent, industrious, sensitive, intensely interested in public policy, and disposed toward collegial efforts. They should have, it would seem, skills in bargaining, in identifying policy alternatives, in weighing costs and gains, and in balancing interests. And they should be "involved" in their tasks and sufficiently motivated and adaptable to win mastery over the legislative process itself. The creative lawmaker, in a word, is at the creative center of the legislative system. His role is active, demanding, and one in which conflict, in all its diversity, is steadily present.

State legislators who meet these standards are apparently too few in number. What appears anomalous is that a great many legislators have no more than faint aspirations to establish themselves as effective lawmakers. Some members by choice, and others by incapacity, leave the critical responsibilities of the legislature to an active minority willing to invest its expertise and other resources to managing the legislative process.

An intensive study by James D. Barber of a group of freshman legislators in the Connecticut legislature, concentrating on their activity in the legislature and their willingness to return for future sessions, suggests that members who assume the role of *lawmaker* are recruited less frequently than is desirable for the legislative system. A strong majority in this sample are described as: *spectators*—passive, submissive, unambitious, preoccupied with watching or applauding, and inclined to see the legislature as "entertaining" and a "wonderful experience"; or *advertisers*—active, upwardly mobile, ambitious, concerned with advertising themselves for career purposes (*e.g.*, law), and inclined to see legislative service as a "golden opportunity" to exhibit their wares; or *reluctants*—passive, motivated by civic duty, occasionally bewildered by events and personalities, repelled by conflict, and tempted to "retreat from politics." Although the strategies and responses of these types are in some respects functional for the system (*e.g.*, "reluctants" help keep down conflict), their contributions to the achievements of the legislature appear marginal when compared with those of the so-called "lawmaker" whose profile was sketched in the opening paragraph.

THE LEGISLATOR AND HIS ENVIRONMENTS

Members who opt for or sink into "secondary" roles in the legislature —who are professionals mainly in the sense that they may be re-elected many times—may have chosen their roles on highly rational grounds, even if assailed by outsiders. With no more than a nod toward the exaggerated language, the argument here is that state legislators perform their functions in hostile, unyielding environments, the effect of which is to erode feelings of responsibility to work steadily in unspectacular legislative tasks. This proposition could as easily be put as a question: Are the rewards sufficiently large for the legislator who tends carefully to the substantive problems of legislation, does his homework, makes a record as an efficient committee member, and participates in the difficult negotiations necessary to settle conflicts?

The Legal-Constitutional Environment. The landscape first recognized by the legislator might be termed the legal-constitutional environment. By and large, it is littered with a number of oppressive facts. Setting aside his regular occupation, the typical legislator is elected to a short term, with low pay but substantial expenses, for a brief session, and given a minimum of technical assistance. He is immersed in a vast sea of existing law, buffeted by thousands of new proposals, and expected to know something about the personnel and programs of a multitude of governmental agencies. Circumstances require him to vote on numerous bills whose actual "sponsors" are unknown, whose purposes seem unclear, whose details seem beyond comprehension, and of whose existence, in fact, he may have been unaware almost until the moment of voting. In most states, the party is not a steady source of cues for making decisions; indeed, the absence of cues is a persistent reason for the tension inherent in the job.

Part of the legislator's struggle is waged against anonymity. He is one of a great many members—one of 400 if he happens to have won a place in the New Hampshire lower house. He is also likely to be an amateur and to find the legislature and its decision-making processes as frustrating as they are bewildering. He soon learns that it is difficult to make any sort of record that could pass for distinctive. He will need several sessions simply to learn the ropes. If other nonlegislative opportunities are available, an investment in several terms may seem too costly, especially since he may lose in a bid for re-election.

Finally, the legislator's creativity is limited because the legislature's creativity is limited. American state constitutions abound with provisions that are not only irrelevant to twentieth century governments but also place heavy procedural and substantive restraints on the powers of the legislature.

The Political Environment. The legislator lives in a political environment unpredictable and threatening. Legislative careers, like most political careers, often are precariously maintained. Even in safe districts, the incumbent may have to face opposition in the primary. And in vigorous two-party districts, legislators move in and out as if in a game of musical chairs. No district is wholly safe for party members on the weak side of a landslide; in 1964, when Barry Goldwater lost overwhelmingly in the presidential race, well over 500 Republican state legislators seeking re-election followed him down the drain.

In some states legislators take office knowing that their stay in the legislature will be short. It is common to find party organizations in multi-county districts following a practice of rotating legislative office among the separate counties. First one county is entitled to the office, then another. Tenure is short for any incumbent. In these circumstances, legislative office appears to be more in the nature of a sinecure than a career, leading one to wonder about the incentives of the transient legislator to perform his legislative work.

No legislator can depend on having an audience of attentive citizens to view his work and record. On the contrary, the chances are overwhelming that no more than a handful of his constituents ever takes account of his voting record. A comprehensive study by Warren E. Miller and Donald E. Stokes of congressional-constituency relations in 116 congressional districts has shown that the typical voter has limited information concerning candidates or issues. About one-half of the *voting* public in these districts had neither read nor heard anything about either candidate for Congress. "Of detailed information about policy stands not more than a chemical trace was found." There is every reason to expect about the same finding in any state legislative system.

For the legislator, political achievements are shared while political risks are individually shouldered. The responsible legislator, no less than the indifferent, finds it difficult to insulate himself from groundswells running against his party. Protecting his career is pretty much his own responsibility. He must deal with interest groups looking for new hostages to take, with restless and demanding constituents in pursuit of indulgences, with actual and potential political opponents, with problems of campaign finance, with the nettlesome problems of patronage distribution, and with local newspapers which tar him when they describe legislators as scarcely a cut above scalawags.

Finally, the job of legislator seems to carry only modest rewards in terms of social or political status. One bit of evidence is that many nominations for legislative office go by default. Much better evidence is that many more legislators voluntarily retire from the legislature than are ever defeated in bids for re-election. Moreover, local political organizations may not place high value on the office. For reasons of this sort, an extended career in the legislature is not a lively option for numerous legislators.

The Legislative Environment. The legislature, like all institutions, is not altogether hospitable to its members. Newcomers must find their way around and learn the "rules of the game." There are problems of winning acceptance and of retaining it. There are admonitions that the best way "to get along is to go along." Here and there the "logroll" is virtually a way of life—the inevitable *quid* in every *quid pro quo*. Sessions may begin in harmony, but it seldom lasts for long. Not infrequently sessions begin in a mood of rancor, brought on by struggles over leadership posts. It takes a long time for the individual legislator to reach his mark, no matter how carefully he tends to business. And most of the time his personal campaigns for legislation, if significant change is involved, end in frustration. Finally, simple arithmetic tells the member that the state legislature may be a dead end in politics. The governor's office, the governor's cabinet, the courts, Congress—there are not enough good jobs to go around and most are subject to the same vicissitudes as his legislative office.

THE MEMBER'S DEMANDS ON THE LEGISLATURE

The argument of these pages is that the legislator's behavior results from certain conditions that intrude on his time, energy, and outlook and establish his priorities. What he does as a legislator is to an important extent the result of his attempts to accommodate to and master hostile environments. Several basic points should be noted to conclude this argument.

The first is that the needs of the legislative system are not identical to the needs of the legislator. Men serve in the legislature for what it offers—measures of power, prestige, deference, self-education, self-gain, a sense of well being, among other things. Superior performance as a legislator is no guarantee that these values will be realized. Indeed, for members who hope to stay in the legislature, "superior performance" may jeopardize the most important value of all, the security that attaches to re-election. Is an excellent record as a lawmaker more instrumental for security than steady personal service to constituents or a generous attitude toward the claims of interest groups? Ordinarily, it may be supposed, nothing has greater claim on the legislator than activities which contribute to his security. Unhappily, the quest for security often does great damage to the reputation of both the legislature and its members. In this regard, mention can be made of gerrymandering in party, area, or individual interest; harassment of the governor as an aid to party; intrusion in city political or administrative affairs; alteration of the local political order as a way of easing re-election; so-called salary "grabs"; patronage disputes; spectacular investigations; and the perennial drive for publicity.

A second point to be noted is that widespread acknowledgment that the legislature has done a good job is not nearly so important to the individual member as recognition that casts him in a favorable light.

Third, the recruitment of American state legislators unquestionably produces a good many who have neither incentive nor flair for major legislative tasks. Errand-running and extolling the institution help rescue them from the oblivion into which they otherwise would tumble.

Fourth, the rewards for conscientious service may easily appear insubstantial to the harassed legislator, since the public knows so little about his record. Believing that the public knows and cares about what its representatives do may be satisfying to democratic theory but believing does not make it so. The realistic legislator is tempted to look for short cuts to security, beginning with reliable service to the constituency and the party organization.

Finally, it seems obvious that legislative performance will suffer so long as legislative service turns out to be, for whatever reasons, merely an interlude for talented men headed in other directions.

Malcolm E. Jewell

3

The Political Setting

A student of the legislature might memorize all of the pertinent constitutional provisions, statutes, and procedural rules and still not understand how the legislature works in practice if he did not understand the political base of legislative power. The sharpest contrasts among state legislatures concern their politics and not their constitutional footing or their rules and procedures. The political base of legislative power has two roots: the apportionment of seats and the nature of two-party competition. A change in the allotment of seats to the counties or in the method of districting within counties may change the balance of political power. A change in the partisan distribution of seats or the establishment of two-party competition in the legislature for the first time may make partisan considerations more important than previously in legislative decision making. The importance of the apportionment and partisan roots of political power becomes obvious in a time of change—and both are undergoing sweeping and unprecedented changes.

The Roots of Legislative Power

BACKGROUND OF MALAPPORTIONMENT

The 1960 census confirmed the population trends that were obvious to any observer of American life. The American people were moving in larger numbers than ever before—from the small towns and farms to the metropolitan centers, and within the metropolis from the core city to the suburbs. The 1960 census documented this trend, but it did not produce a legislative stampede toward up-to-date, population-based appor-

MALCOLM E. JEWELL *is Professor of Political Science at the University of Kentucky. He has been a Visiting Associate Professor at Duke University and is the author of many publications, including* The State Legislatures: Politics and Practice, The Politics of Reapportionment, *and* Senatorial Politics and Policy.

tionments. It might be true that rural dwellers were less isolated and less suspicious of the city folk than before and that the increasingly diverse interests in the legislature were seldom arrayed in opposition along simple urban-rural lines. But legislative majorities preferred the status quo; it protected the political careers of incumbent legislators and at the same time served the interests of those groups having effective access to the legislative majority.

There are many ways of measuring the malapportionment that existed following the 1960 census and prior to judicial intervention. The House districts in Vermont that varied from 35,000 to 38 persons and the Senate districts in California that ranged from 6 million to 14,000 population are dramatic extremes but not useful measuring sticks. It is more helpful to know that one-third of the voters from the smallest districts could elect a majority in more than one-half of the upper houses and two-fifths of the lower houses. Less than one-fifth of the voters could elect a majority in either or both houses of fourteen states. These are theoretical majorities. It is more meaningful to measure the balance of urban and rural apportionment. In both Florida and New Jersey, for example, a majority of the population resided in five counties but had only one-eighth to one-fourth, respectively, of the Senate seats.

The clearest device for measuring malapportionment is the "value of the vote" enjoyed by citizens in counties of various sizes. The calculations by Paul T. David and Ralph Eisenberg showed that in 1960 the value of the vote (which would be 100 on the basis of "one man, one vote") ranged from 76 in all counties of over half a million population taken together to 171 in all counties of under 25,000 as a group. In some states the contrast was much greater between the largest and smallest categories of counties; in Florida, the value of the vote ranged from 16 to 476. There were also sharp contrasts in the value of the vote between urban and suburban counties. It was close to 100 in some urban counties like New York and Philadelphia, but was much lower in many of the suburban counties, as well as in counties that were mixtures of urban and suburban, such as Fulton, Georgia (12), and Dallas, Texas (40). In Maryland, the value of the vote was 82 in Baltimore city but only 26 in suburban Baltimore county.

EFFECTS OF MALAPPORTIONMENT

What difference did it make? The most obvious effect in many states was on the partisan makeup of the legislature. In most of the northeastern and midwestern states the Democratic party gained a majority position in the large cities during the New Deal, while the Republicans maintained their dominant position in most of the rural counties. From 1932 to 1962 the apportionment system usually preserved Republican control of one or both houses, despite frequent Democratic successes in the gubernatorial elections of many of these states. Divided government could not be attributed entirely to apportionment; in some states Democratic legislative votes were "wasted" because they were concentrated in a few urban counties and were thinly scattered elsewhere. But Democratic governors in most northern states had reason to echo Governor Alfred E. Smith's complaint that the New York legislature was "constitutionally Republican." Malapportionment has had a less publicized effect in some of the border and southwestern states which were traditionally Democratic and where recent Republican successes in metropolitan counties have not been translated into many legislative seats.

The effects of malapportionment on public policy are not so obvious and have been the subject of debate among political scientists as well as among political leaders. The analysis of "what might have been" is a frustrating exercise for the political scientist who is striving for precision in his research. It is possible to compare past voting records of urban and rural legislators, but it is not possible to determine how these legislators would have voted had the rural majority in the legislature been smaller, or what additional bills would have emerged from committees that were not completely under rural control. However, a few speculative conclusions may be suggested in speculative fashion. It is unusual in any legislature to find a vote taken on which all the metropolitan legislators vote in opposition to all the non-metropolitan legislators, and such votes would probably be just as unusual in a legislature where apportionment was based on population. Metropolitan legislators represent a variety of constituents with conflicting viewpoints and interests, and the same is true of rural legislators. Some of the issues that most directly concern metropolitan counties, such as annexation and zoning legislation, are likely to arouse greater controversy within metropolitan counties than between these and rural counties.

Although urban and rural legislators do not instinctively man opposing barricades when the roll is called, their attitudes have been different in most legislatures on many issues of importance. Voting records probably minimize these differences because the outnumbered urban legislators have compromised in order to win concessions from the rural majority. In recent decades the legislative record of action or inaction on labor and welfare issues, or civil rights and segregation, for example, would probably have been different in some states under a different apportionment. Some of the states in which malapportionment has deprived the Democratic party of legislative majorities are ones in which both parties often vote with a high degree of cohesion on major issues. In such cases the direct effect of apportionment on political parties would bring about an indirect effect on policy. The tactics of Democratic governors would have been different and their programs might have been bolder had they enjoyed a Democratic majority. Ten or twenty years ago reapportionment would probably have meant more Democratic majorities and more liberal legislation in many northern states, but the partisan and policy consequences of reapportionment today are less predictable because it is the suburbs that are gaining population most rapidly.

The widespread, discernible, and probably the most important effect of malapportionment on legislation has been the impact on state aid to local government. The formulas used for distributing state funds for roads, education, and other purposes have frequently given disproportionate weight to area and little weight to population. In some states a portion of the gasoline tax has been allocated to rural roads, but little state help has been available to meet the problems of metropolitan counties being strangled by traffic. In some extreme cases certain state funds have been distributed equally to all counties, whatever their population. This was the case of the race-track revenues in Florida, which met over half of the local revenue needs in some counties but were of negligible help in the metropolitan counties. Malapportionment has had other more subtle consequences within the legislature. The recruitment of leaders, the structure of committees, the tactics of lobbyists, and many other characteristics of the legislative system have presumably been affected in ways that remain obscure but suggest the difficulty of defining precisely the policy implications of any apportionment.

JUDICIAL INTERVENTION IN APPORTIONMENT

It was probably inevitable that urban interests, so long underrepresented in the legislature, would turn to other political arenas in an effort to accomplish their purposes. Ever since the advent of the New Deal, these interests have sought, with considerable success, to win federal support for urban programs. But in the modern federal system, state support is necessary if federal programs are to be fully implemented. Urban interests discovered that their objectives could not be accomplished by simply bypassing the state legislature.

The judicial arena offered an opportunity for challenging the apportionment that ensured rural control of so many legislatures. Although there was precedent in the state courts for invalidating apportionments, state judges had not been willing to require the enactment of new apportionments which would meet constitutional standards. In many states there was little reason to seek state judicial action because malapportionment was constitutionally enshrined. The United States Supreme Court, on the other hand, had shown an increasing interest in removing obstacles to the right to vote and had even invalidated a districting law that had a discriminatory effect on Negroes (*Gomillion v. Lightfoot*).

The Supreme Court decided in March 1962 (*Baker v. Carr*) that a citizen's rights under the equal protection clause of the Fourteenth Amendment might be infringed if malapportionment was so serious as to constitute "invidious discrimination" and that the Court would exercise jurisdiction in such a case. By failing to specify constitutional standards for apportionment, the Supreme Court in effect invited state and federal courts to devise standards that were appropriate to particular states.

The resulting decisions of lower courts produced more confusion than consensus about the standards to be met by state legislatures engaged in reapportionment. The confusion ended abruptly in June 1964 when the Supreme Court handed down its decisions in a number of apportionment cases, notably *Reynolds v. Sims*. The Court said that both branches of a state legislature must consist of districts that are "as nearly of equal population as is practicable." The Court declared that there was "no constitutional difference" between the two houses. It rejected the validity of referendums on apportionment on the grounds that a majority of the people cannot be permitted to infringe a citizen's constitutional rights. The Court recognized that mathematical exactness was not a "workable constitutional requirement" and refused to endorse any mathematical formula for acceptable limits of equality, but it served notice that any apportionment plan incorporating large-scale variations from population equality would be viewed with suspicion. The principle of using counties and cities as the basis for creating districts was acceptable only so long as it did not necessitate a serious departure from the principle of equal population.

The Supreme Court has undertaken to determine whether legislative apportionments meet the standards of the equal protection clause, a constitutional provision that has traditionally been used to protect individual voting rights. The Court has used the phrase "one person, one vote" in describing its standard of equality, and it has emphasized the rights of individual citizens in rejecting the argument that voters can impose an inequitable apportionment by referendum. The Court appears to have perceived the apportionment cases as *"simply one more round of civil rights cases in the field of voting rights,"* as Robert G. Dixon, Jr., asserted in an address at an American Assembly cosponsored by The George Washington University in May 1965, on *The Congress and America's Future*. Dixon argues that the Court has confused the objective of individual equality with that of fair representation of the various groups in a society. Justice Frankfurter, in his dissenting opinion in the *Baker* case, stated: "What is actually being asked of the Court in this case is to choose among competing bases of representation—ultimately, really, among competing theories of political philosophy. . . ." A majority of the Court evidently believed that the problem before it was the simpler and narrower one of distributing the voters as equally as possible among districts.

It is important to make clear what the Court has, and has not, done. It has required that a high degree of equality in the population of districts in both houses of the legislature be established and be maintained in accord with population changes revealed by the census. Although there is room for some variation from state to state in conforming to this principle, it is clear that deviations from population equality will not be large enough to have any significant effect on legislative politics.

The Court has not reached any decisions about the system of representation. It has not required that the legislature be divided into single-member or multi-member districts. It has not asserted that gerrymandering is unconstitutional. It has not determined that any apportionment infringes the constitutional rights of political parties or of particular racial or nationality groups. Cases have reached the Supreme Court that have touched on all these problems, but the Court has yet to seize the opportunity to assert any such standards for fair representation. Judicial efforts to protect the rights of *groups* to fair representation would represent a departure from the Court's concentration on *individual* voting rights and would lead the Court deeper into the "political thicket" foreseen by Justice Frankfurter. But in January 1965 (*Fortson v. Dorsey*) the Court hinted that it might be prepared to engage in just such a venture:

> It might well be that, designedly or otherwise, a multi-member constituency apportionment scheme, under the circumstances of a particular case, would operate to minimize or cancel out the voting strength of racial or political elements of the voting population.

TWO-PARTY COMPETITION IN THE LEGISLATURE

One of the most important consequences of reapportionment will be to accelerate changes that are already under way in the nature of partisan competition in the legislatures. The scale of state interparty competition used by Ranney (cited in Chapter 1) is based on the proportion of legislative seats and the percentage of the gubernatorial vote won by each party and also the percentage of time that the governorship and the two legislative branches were controlled by each party. Legislative parties are likely to have greater importance if control of the legislature alternates over a period of time, but even if there is little or no alternation, parties may be significant in states where the minority party consistently has a large proportion of legislative seats. Also, frequent turnover and close contests in gubernatorial elections are likely to increase the spirit of partisanship in the legislature.

We can define legislative competition more narrowly by determining which legislatures have had two parties and in which ones the parties have both had periods of majority control. The eleven southern states can be described as having one-party legislatures. In five of these (Alabama, Arkansas, Louisiana, Mississippi, and South Carolina) Democratic dominance of the legislature is complete and a Republican legislator remains a rarity. In the other six southern states the Democratic party consistently maintains solid control of the legislature but there is a recognizable legislative minority. In North Carolina, Tennessee, and Virginia a small group of Republicans have been elected for many years from traditional Republican districts in the mountains. The Republican legislative party has emerged only recently in Florida, Georgia, and Texas, with its members coming primarily from metropolitan districts.

There are eight more states in which the legislature has been controlled consistently by one party since World War II, but in each case the minority party has occasionally elected a governor and has maintained substantial strength in the legislature. Five of these are under Democratic control (Arizona, Kentucky, Maryland, Oklahoma, and West Virginia) and three are Republican (Kansas, New Hampshire, and Vermont). Two states, Nebraska and Minnesota, have nonpartisan legislatures. Alaska and Hawaii are excluded from this analysis.

In the remaining twenty-seven states the legislature may be defined as a two-party one. In each of these states, from 1947 through 1966, majority control of one or both houses of the legislature alternated between the two parties and (except for Missouri) there was some alternation in control of the governorship. Throughout all or most of the twenty-year period there were two viable parties in these legislatures. In sixteen of these legislatures, however, one of the parties had a legislative majority in both houses during at least 14 of the 20 years. Despite close gubernatorial contests and partly as a result of malapportionment, strong Democratic legislative parties remained in the minority throughout most of this period in both houses of the Illinois, Michigan, New Jersey, New York, and Ohio legislatures. Another group of legislatures in which one party usually had control were ones in which two-party competition had been increasing and only later became strong enough for the minority party to win an occasional legislative majority. The growth of competition is likely to make the balance of power between the legislative parties closer in two-party states, as well as to increase the number of two-party states.

The number of states with competitive party systems grew slowly but steadily after the New Deal. The first effects of the New Deal were felt in the major industrial states of the northeast and midwest, where the Democratic party developed, or revived, a solid base of strength in the metropolitan areas and began to compete on even terms with the Republicans. In the 1950s the Democratic party began to win statewide elections in a number of the less industrialized states of the North, both because of growing urbanization and because of its increasing success in the farm areas. The Republican invasion of the South and the border states, initiated by Eisenhower in 1952, did not at first have much impact on state politics. But in later years the Republican party began to establish an organizational base, particularly in metropolitan areas, and to run candidates for statewide and legislative offices. The revival of state Democratic parties in the North and Republican parties in the South resulted from the trends of presidential politics, but in both cases there was a time lag between a minority party's success in national and state elections.

There is an additional time lag in the establishment of competitive legislative parties, which may be caused by one or more factors. When a party first wins the governorship after a long period as the minority party it is rarely able to win a majority of legislative seats, perhaps not even in one house. Several factors may explain this lag. In order to generate legislative candidates throughout the state, a party needs the kind of widespread organizational strength that takes time to develop. It is not unusual for a party to make a serious bid for the governorship while running candidates for less than half of the legislative seats. A party that has long been in the minority finds it difficult to attract legislative candidates who are able enough and sufficiently well known to win at the polls. When a minority party makes a breakthrough, it is often because its gubernatorial candidate is unusually popular; voters who break traditional habits to vote for him may see no reason to support his legislative running mates. In some states a minority party has enough voting strength to elect a governor, but this strength is so heavily concentrated in a few areas, such as metropolitan districts, that under the single-member district system it wastes votes and is unable to elect a legislative majority. Finally, and most important, the apportionment system in most states has resulted in the underrepresentation of those metropolitan areas in which the minority parties—the Democrats in the North and the Republicans in the South—have amassed their greatest strength. As we have noted, malapportionment has handicapped the Democratic party in many northern states long after the Democrats achieved a position of strength in gubernatorial elections equaling or surpassing that of the Republicans.

Election returns in the 1960s provide evidence of closer party competition for legislative seats. In five of the state legislatures that we have labeled two-party the Democratic party won control of one or both houses for the first time in the postwar period in the 1964 election: Iowa, Maine, Michigan, New York, and North Dakota. Republican candidates competed for only a handful of Texas' legislative seats in 1956 but for about half of them in 1962 and 1964; the percentage of seats with Republican candidates in Louisiana rose from none in 1952 to 17 in 1964, and in South Carolina it rose from none in 1960 to 24 in 1964; in Florida and Georgia the number of successful Republican candidates in metropolitan counties increased sharply. Although in 1966 it is too early to gauge the full effects of reapportionment, it contributed, for example, to recent Democratic victories in Michigan, New Jersey, and New York, and to Republican gains in Florida and Georgia.

Trends and Consequences of Reapportionment

The Supreme Court's decision in the *Baker* case precipitated suits in the courts of a large majority of states challenging the constitutionality of legislative apportionments. In most of these cases the courts found the existing apportionments to be unconstitutional. Those lower courts that

upheld apportionments were often overruled by subsequent decisions of
the Supreme Court. Most lower court judges have been reluctant to
undertake the task of devising new apportionments to replace ones that
they have found unconstitutional. They have recognized that the creation
of districts among and within counties necessitates political decisions that
the judges do not want to make. The usual judicial procedure has been
to give the legislature a fixed amount of time for enacting a new apportionment and then to decide the constitutionality of the new law. In
some states the courts have held the new apportionments to be constitutional. Where these apportionments still fell short of judicial standards,
the courts have sometimes given the legislatures a second opportunity or
—if an election was impending—have permitted the apportionment to
take effect temporarily and have given the new legislature a deadline for
enacting a better apportionment. Only in a few cases, when an election
was impending and the legislative enactment fell far short of constitutional standards, have the courts selected an apportionment plan and
ordered it to take effect.

LEGISLATIVE RESISTANCE AND ACCOMMODATION

These judicial tactics have placed a heavy burden on the legislatures.
Most legislators would prefer to do the job of reapportionment in order
to give maximum possible protection to the personal and political interests that might be ignored by the courts; but this preference has not
made the job any less unpleasant or difficult. Judicial initiative has forced
legislators to devise plans of apportionment that jeopardize or destroy
the political careers of themselves or their fellow members and that require their own counties to lose representation. Political parties or factions have been forced to enact apportionments that threaten their majority position in the legislature. It is not surprising that legislators
resent these pressures, nor is it difficult to understand why they usually
have tried to devise an apportionment formula satisfactory to the courts
while doing as little damage as possible to political and personal interests.
Initially the guidelines provided by the courts were neither clear nor
consistent, and legislators were able to cite judicial decisions in one state
or another that seemed to permit minimum accommodation to the principle of one man, one vote.

Some legislatures tried to preserve the practice of guaranteeing a seat
in one house to each county, despite the gross disparities in district population that often resulted. Others have adopted the population principle
in one house but made the other house less representative than previously, in some cases even giving each county equal representation in
the second house. This practice, sometimes referred to as the "federal
plan," was sanctioned by some lower courts between 1962 and 1964. In
some cases, constitutional amendments on apportionment that fell far

short of population equality in one or both houses were submitted to popular vote. Some of these plans were rejected at the polls, but it was hoped that the courts would not invalidate any that had popular approval. However, the Supreme Court's decisions in June of 1964 made it clear that none of these devices would be upheld. Since then there has been no doubt about the constitutional standard that the legislatures must follow: Districts in both houses must be drawn as nearly equal in population as is practical and reapportionments must be carried out at least every ten years to maintain this equality.

At the time of the *Reynolds* decision in 1964 only a few states had devised apportionments clearly consistent with the newly announced standards. Since that time a number of legislative reapportionment plans have been accepted by the courts. In Tennessee, where the federal court had repeatedly reviewed apportionment laws and declared them only temporarily valid, the Baker case was finally concluded in November of 1965 with judicial approval of a new apportionment. In several states, such as Indiana and New York, the legislature solved the problem of predicting judicial standards by passing a series of apportionment laws at one time and letting the court choose one that it considered satisfactory.

Lower court decisions have confronted some state legislatures with more rigid standards for apportionment. Some lower courts have criticized the use of both single- and multi-member districts or the use of floterial districts in a legislative chamber; some have tried to prohibit partisan or racial gerrymandering; some have challenged the practice of basing districts on county lines when the result was inequalities in population; and some have set a maximum percentage limit on deviations in the population of districts. To date, none of these stricter standards has been adopted by the Supreme Court. Some legislatures have been confronted by conflicting decisions of federal and state courts, but the Supreme Court has given preference in such cases to the federal decision.

In some states the legislators have found themselves trapped between the requirements of federal courts and the provisions of state constitutions. Without doubt, the apportionment provisions of state constitutions are invalid when they conflict with the requirements of the federal constitution. But it is not clear to what extent legislatures may disregard state constitutions in attempting to devise apportionments that are both equitable and acceptable to a majority of legislators. State courts must decide, for example, whether the legislature may disregard constitutional provisions that limit the size of the legislature or that prohibit the division of a county into legislative districts.

LEGISLATIVE CHALLENGE TO THE COURTS

At the same time that state legislatures were adopting apportionment laws in an effort to comply with the one man, one vote principle adopted by the Supreme Court in 1964, a majority of them were seeking an amendment to the United States Constitution that would exempt one house of the legislature from that requirement. The campaign to petition Congress to call a constitutional convention for this purpose picked up momentum in southern and western states early in 1965 when most legislatures were in regular session, but the resistance of legislatures in the northeast and midwest was strong enough to stall the drive, short of the necessary thirty-four states.

Although the legislative campaign to petition Congress failed, a parallel drive within Congress came closer to success. Many congressmen were disturbed by the drastic changes in the power balance in their state that they foresaw resulting from the one man, one vote principle. Others were critical of the federal courts because of the speed with which they were acting and the rigidity of judicial standards for apportionment. It was obvious from congressional debate that many congressmen were voting to reverse or limit the Court's apportionment decisions in order to express their resentment of the Court's decisions on a wide variety of topics. The objective of "putting the Court in its place" was evident in a bill that would have removed all jurisdiction of both the federal district courts and the Supreme Court over apportionment. During the summer of 1964 the bill passed the House by a vote of 218-175, but a similar measure was defeated in the Senate.

During the same session of Congress a liberal filibuster in the Senate blocked a measure that would have delayed implementation of the judicial decisions on apportionment in order to prevent the disruption of state election machinery and (as its sponsors freely admitted) to give Congress time to consider a constitutional amendment before reapportionment of all legislative bodies had become an established fact. During the 1965 session the Senate focused its attention on a constitutional amendment, proposed by Senator Everett Dirksen, which would have permitted the voters of a state to approve apportionment of one legislative house according to factors other than population. The proposed amendment won the support of a majority of senators but not by the necessary two-thirds margin, in the House the measure remained stalled in the Judiciary Committee.

The efforts to limit the effects of the Supreme Court's decisions on legislative apportionment almost succeeded, because the political forces adversely affected by these decisions were strongly represented both in Washington and in the state capitals. These efforts failed because the urban interests that expected to gain from reapportionment constituted a powerful minority in Washington and held a majority in a number of states. As the balance of legislative power continues to change in the wake of judicial decisions, these urban interests become increasingly capable of blocking any amendment to the federal constitution that would dilute the principle of one man, one vote.

EFFECTS ON PARTY COMPETITION

The short-run effects of reapportionment on party strength in specific state legislatures are not difficult to determine. These anticipated effects have spurred the opposition to reapportionment, and some of these effects have already been felt. Most immediately, the Democratic party will gain in many northeastern and midwestern states, and for some states, in some elections, these gains will provide the margin necessary for a Democratic majority in one or both houses of the legislature. In those southern and border states where Republican strength is concentrated in metropolitan areas the potential Republican gain from reapportionment is just as great, but it may be less immediate because in some of these states the party still lacks the organizational strength to capitalize on reapportionment.

Reapportionment will affect intraparty as well as interparty power. In many states control of the Republican party has already begun to shift from the small towns and farms to the cities and suburbs. Reapportionment will accelerate this trend. Throughout the South the rural dominance of Democratic parties is threatened both by reapportionment and by the development of an organized bloc of Negro voters, who are most effective in the metropolitan areas. The legislative party is only one component of a state party, but it is an important component; changes in the legislative party will have repercussions throughout the political system.

The long-run political effects of reapportionment are less predictable because it is suburbia that is gaining population and suburban political trends are difficult to foresee. The suburb has confounded political prognosticators, and the suburban voter has been more often stereotyped than analyzed. There is no reason to expect political trends to be common to suburbs representing a wide variety of socio-economic levels. One common characteristic of suburbs is their lack of political traditions; as our population grows more mobile, suburbs are likely to be composed of voters who come from a variety of political environments. In short, reapportionment will mean that fewer legislators represent districts traditionally dominated by one party, whether rural counties or districts in the core cities of metropolitan areas; more legislators will come from districts where two-party competition is likely to be high.

Research has demonstrated that two-party competition for legislative seats is greater in metropolitan counties (except for some of the core cities) than in the more rural counties. Similarly, there is evidence that primary competition within the parties is greater in metropolitan areas, except where there is a party organization strong enough to dominate the nominating process. It is also true that increased two-party competition may reduce primary competition within the previously dominant party. We may conclude that reapportionment will result in an increasing proportion of legislators facing substantial competition in either the primary or the general election, or perhaps both. Whatever the effects of reapportionment on voluntary retirement, it is likely to occasion an increasing rate of involuntary retirement from the legislature.

EFFECTS ON RURAL REPRESENTATION

Obviously, reapportionment is going to decrease the proportion of members from the small, rural counties in all states, but it has other ramifications for rural representation. In about half of the states each county has had at least one member in the lower house, but in many of these states this will no longer be possible unless the membership of the House is increased, perhaps drastically. In those legislatures that enact many local bills by ratifying the decisions of members from the county involved, such a change in the base of representation will necessitate a change in the method of handling local legislation.

In any state where the House member is forced to represent more than a single county a change in role can be expected. It is possible that some legislators will become less locally oriented and more conscious of state-wide problems. Frequent reapportionments and the use of districts with many counties will reduce the practice in some legislatures of rotating a member among the several counties in a district. Some rural legislators, particularly in the Senate, will face a problem of communicating with constituents because their districts will span several thousand square miles and include a large number of sparsely populated counties. As this problem becomes more acute there is likely to be pressure for increasing the size of the Senate in order to reduce the number of counties that individual senators represent.

Some legislatures have given serious consideration to another solution for this problem—the use of weighted votes that would either give rural legislators a fraction of a vote or give urban legislators more than a single vote. Such an approach creates more problems than it solves with regard to the weight of votes in committees and caucuses, the method of making committee assignments, and the power exercised by committee chairmen and other legislative leaders. Moreover, it seems to be based on the premise that legislators are nothing more than delegates from their districts or human voting machines. It is difficult to imagine how a legislator with only half a vote could be made half as persuasive in debate, half as effective in committee work and informal negotiations, or half as accessible to lobbyists.

DISTRICTING METHODS IN METROPOLITAN COUNTIES

Every decennial census shows that an increasing proportion of the population is concentrated in a few metropolitan counties. In 1960 half of the population of such states as California, Florida, Illinois, Ohio, and Pennsylvania was found in no more than seven of the state's counties.

We can expect the 1970 census to show this pattern continuing. For the first time in our history these population trends are beginning to be fully reflected in the apportionment of legislative seats. As an increasing proportion of the legislators are chosen from a few large counties the problems of creating and adjusting districts within the metropolitan counties become as important as the more publicized matter of apportioning seats to the counties.

In such states as California, Kentucky, New York, Rhode Island, and Wisconsin, large counties are divided into single-member districts. A large county may, instead, be divided into several multi-member districts, each electing a few members—perhaps three, four, or five. This has been done in Maryland, Michigan, Oregon, and Washington, for example. A third possibility is to use the entire county as a multi-member district. This was the practice in parts of the North and in almost every southern county that elected more than one representative prior to the Baker decision.

It would be possible also to combine two or more districting methods in a single county; the new apportionment adopted in Georgia in 1965, for example, provides for the election of some members at large and some in single-member districts in large counties. Whenever one or more multi-member districts are used in a county a distinction should be made between the "place" method (under which each candidate must designate for which place or position he is running) and the "free-for-all" method (under which all candidates run against each other). A final possibility is the use of some method of proportional representation in the metropolitan county. This is used only in the Illinois House, which has a cumulative voting system. The House is divided into three-man districts (throughout the state and not just in Cook county), and the minority party is usually able to elect one of the three.

Paul T. David and Ralph Eisenberg calculated the proportion of legislators elected by different methods in all counties in the United States that chose more than one senator or representative (not only metropolitan counties) prior to the Baker decision. Two-thirds of the senators were chosen in single-member districts, and one-third were chosen in countywide multi-member districts. Slightly over one-third of the representatives were elected by each of these methods, and less than one-third were elected in multi-member districts that were smaller than the entire county. The trend since the Baker decision has been to increase the proportion of single-member districts and to decrease the proportion of countywide multi-member districts as the number of legislators elected from metropolitan counties has grown.

Some of the consequences of various districting methods are obvious and some remain uncertain because not enough research has been done on the representative process in metropolitan counties. The most obvious disadvantage of the countywide multi-member district in a large county is the long ballot that confronts the voter. For example, the selection of eighteen members to the Ohio House has presented the voter in Cuyahoga County with an awesome task. The problem has been even more serious in large southern counties where the primary is the decisive election and the voter cannot solve his problem by voting a straight party ticket. The voters of Jefferson County, Alabama, had to choose seven members of the House from 33 candidates in the 1962 primary and, as a result of reapportionment, later that year had to select 10 more from a total of 51 candidates. The same year there were 52 candidates in the primary for nine House seats in Davidson County, Tennessee.

POLITICAL CONSEQUENCES OF METROPOLITAN DISTRICTING

A metropolitan county is composed of various parties, interests, and racial and ethnic groups; and an essential problem of districting is to provide adequate representation for each of these. Any method of districting other than proportional representation wastes the votes of the minority party and consequently benefits the majority party. In a county divided into single-member districts it would be possible for a second party to poll only a minority of votes in each, but if the minority party has pockets of strength in the county it is likely to carry some districts. If the county is divided into several multi-member districts, the minority party must have larger concentrations of strength in order to win a district. In either case, the majority party may maximize its advantage by gerrymandering.

If the county is not divided into districts, and if straight-ticket voting is common, all of the minority party's votes are likely to be wasted and the legislative delegation is likely to be composed entirely of majority party members. The frequency of straight-party voting and the lopsided partisan balance in most multi-member districts are suggested by a survey of all multi-member districts in Indiana, Michigan, Pensylvania, and West Virginia during several elections in the 1950s. Out of 338 district elections (in which over 900 legislators were elected) there were only 13 elections in which a legislative delegation was chosen that included members from both parties.

Party interests are not the only ones affected by the method of districting. The Negro voter is becoming an increasingly potent force in metropolitan areas, North and South. Because Negroes are concentrated in certain parts of metropolitan counties and because they remain a numerical minority in most such counties, they usually have a better chance to elect one or more legislators (white or Negro) who are responsive to their needs if a county is divided into districts. Some of the controversy over dividing southern metropolitan counties into legislative districts has been directly related to the question of Negro representation. Negro voters may be more cohesive and more concentrated geographically than others, but the problem of representation concerns all residents of the metropolis. The slum dwellers (white or Negro), retired persons living in older sections, and suburbanites (of various income levels) all want representatives in the legislature who are familiar with and sympathetic to their needs. Some of the most important organized groups in a metropolitan county, such as business and labor organizations, may not have a constituent base concentrated in any single part of the county.

There is one important difference in the representation process between political parties and other interests. The votes for a political party are wasted, as the term is used, unless they are sufficiently concentrated in a district to elect a legislator. An interest group, whether organized or unorganized, does not have to command a majority in any particular district to influence the nomination and election of legislators. By providing the balance of power or cooperating with other groups, a group may help to determine the outcome of the election and may, as a consequence, gain access to the legislator. Under some conditions, for example, Negro voters might have broader influence on a county's legislative delegation if they were able to join with others to elect a slate in a countywide district, or if they had minority strength in a number of single-member districts instead of having a majority in a few single-member districts. Evaluation of districting schemes involves not only what is fair but what effect a particular districting will have on various interests. The leaders of an organized group may disagree on the tactics to be followed when districting legislation is being drafted.

METROPOLITAN DISTRICTING AND THE REPRESENTATIVE SYSTEM

The method of districting affects the representative system in a variety of other ways, that in the absence of research can be suggested only tentatively. The member who is elected from a single-member district may become the spokesman for a few narrow interests. He may be able to maintain personal contact with his constituents, although he is likely to be handicapped in publicizing his actions because he gets little attention in the news media that cover the entire metropolis. The legislative candidate who must run countywide is more likely to need support from a political organization or from major interest groups because of the costs of campaigning and the breadth of voter support that he needs. Once elected, he must serve a wider and perhaps often conflicting variety of constituent interests, but he may be more visible to constituents through the news media. We know very little about the ways in which organized interests seek access to metropolitan legislators. Do they seek out only those members representing a district where that group has numerical strength? Does a member try to represent only his single district, or the whole county? Does he know exactly which interests are represented in his district? If he is a Republican, does he respond sympathetically to requests from Republican voters in other parts of the county who are represented by Democrats? Although the representative process in metro-

politan areas is imperfectly understood, and the effect of districting upon
it is even less clear, it cannot be doubted that the effect of districting is
important.

The countywide district has substantial disadvantages: the ballot is
long, the costs of campaigning are high, a one-party delegation is likely
to be elected, and major interests may be poorly represented. A multitude
of single-member districts has other disadvantages: the districts may become grossly unequal in the ten years following a census, frequent redistricting may be chaotic and vulnerable to gerrymandering, legislators
may represent only narrow interests, and there may be no one capable of
viewing the county's problems as a whole.

It would be easier to prescribe a districting formula if we knew more
about the effects of various districting schemes, but the disadvantages of
both extremes are serious enough to suggest that we need more experi-
ments with balanced districting methods. There is precedent for electing
members in a metropolitan county at large in one house and by single-
member districts in the other, or combining the two techniques in one
branch of the legislature. This technique provides representation to both
broad and narrow interests in the county, but it may combine some of the
disadvantages of both methods. Another practice that has been used is
the establishment of a number of small districts (electing three, four, or
five members) in a county. If it were possible to divide a county into
natural boundaries of some kind these could remain unchanged (and not
subject to gerrymandering) while the number of members in each district
varied with population changes. Even if this were not feasible, the use
of several multi-member districts would minimize the problem of drawing
and redrawing boundaries. It might ensure that major political interests
in the county were represented without making each legislator a spokesman for a single narrow interest, and it might establish a reasonable
maximum limit to both the length of the ballot and the costs of legislative campaigns.

The problem of legislative representation within the metropolis will
become increasingly important. Although it is too early to suggest a
definitive formula, it is timely to suggest the need for research and the
desirability of experimenting with various formulas. Any method of districting that does not discriminate blatantly against a major political
interest in the metropolis would seem to deserve consideration.

THE PROSPECTS FOR UNICAMERALISM

One of the most intriguing questions that arose in the wake of the
Supreme Court's Reynolds decision in 1964 was whether this requirement
for a population base in both houses would rekindle interest in unicameralism. The topic was debated in legislative halls and in the press
for several years after Nebraska adopted unicameralism in 1934, but in
recent years even reformers and political scientists seemed to have lost

interest in the question. Historically bicameralism was developed in this country as a means for permitting diverse interests to be separately represented. Most of the colonies separated the elected members and those appointed by the governor into two houses, and most early state constitutions provided for a bicameral legislature, although Vermont used a single house until 1836.

The early senates protected the interests of property through property qualifications for voting, which persisted in many states until the era of Jacksonian democracy. In modern times the two houses have represented substantially different interests only in those states where the apportionment gave substantially greater weight to population in one house than in the other; on the eve of the Baker decision only about one-third of the states were in this category. A few states relied primarily on a population base for apportionment in both houses, and a larger number left the cities seriously underrepresented in both houses. Although the contrast between Senate and House apportionment in the past has been exaggerated, the use of a population base in both does provide an opportunity for a new look at unicameralism, and this subject has recently been studied carefully in several states.

The Supreme Court in the Reynolds case explicitly rejected the suggestion that it was making bicameralism "anachronistic and meaningless." There are important differences between the representative systems in the two branches that are likely to continue. In every state the lower house is a larger body, and consequently its members usually represent smaller constituencies than do senators. The use of multi-member districts in one house and single-member districts in the other would have a similar effect in varying the size of constituencies. In more than half of the legislatures senators serve a longer term than representatives. In short, bicameralism permits a state to add a variety of dimensions to its representative system, but this does not necessarily mean that every state will consider such variety essential.

The difficulties of evaluating unicameralism arise from the fact that in modern times it has been used only in Nebraska. The Nebraska experiment demonstrates that a unicameral legislature can be run with remarkable efficiency, free from the deadlocks, logjams, and recurrent crises that plague most state legislatures. In Nebraska, procedures have been devised to assure careful deliberation, well publicized public hearings, and ample time for debate on the floor before a vote is taken. Such procedures provide an answer to the fears that have been repeatedly expressed since the time when John Adams warned: "A single assembly is liable to all the vices, follies, and frailties of an individual; subject to fits of humor, starts of passion, flights of enthusiasm, partialities or prejudice, and consequently productive of hasty results and absurd judgments." To anyone who has experienced the chaos that frequently marks the closing days of a busy legislative session, Adams' description seems just as appropriate to a bicameral legislature. Bills may be passed by the second house with little scrutiny because one house has already acted, while other measures may be rejected at the last moment because there is not time enough to work out compromises or may simply be trampled to death in the rush for adjournment. Of course, unicameralism does not guarantee careful scrutiny of bills such as has been the practice in Nebraska. In a larger state with a heavier legislative workload or in a legislature dominated by strong party leadership, there would be greater risk of precipitate action. The Nebraska experience simply shows that there are procedural devices more effective than a bicameral system for encouraging legislative deliberation.

The Nebraska experiment is of limited value as an example for other states because Nebraska is a state with a small population that has largely escaped the problems of metropolitan growth and ethnic diversity that are familiar to the more industrial states. Legislative politics in Nebraska are low-pressure, nonpartisan, and orderly; but this is not primarily a consequence of unicameralism. It is difficult to envisage how unicameralism would work if it were transplanted to California, Florida, or New York; it might have a different effect in each state. In any state the use of a unicameral system should make it easier to pass legislation—good or bad. Those interest groups seeking legislative action would have to win the support of a smaller number of leaders and committee members; and the advantage that always seems to be enjoyed in our complex legislative system by the opponents of legislation would be reduced. It is possible that a single house would be more responsible to the voter because there would be less reason for deadlock and buck-passing and because the legislative structure—being simpler—would be more visible to the voter and more easily understood by him.

The advocates of unicameralism often propose that membership in a single house be small enough to make it feasible to pay substantially higher salaries and to raise the prestige of the office in an attempt to attract better men into legislative service. There is already a trend toward higher pay, better staff services, and longer sessions, but it is doubtful whether in a bicameral system it would be feasible to make legislators into full-time professionals, like congressmen. This would be more feasible in a small unicameral body. It should be kept in mind, however, that establishment of a small single chamber would accelerate the sharp drop in the number of representatives for rural counties that has been occasioned by reapportionment.

It is always necessary, in discussing state legislatures, to remember the diversity of states. The needs of Texas and Vermont, of New Mexico and New York, are vastly different. It is possible that a unicameral legislature would be as successful in some states as it appears to have been in Nebraska but would not fit the needs of other states, particularly those with large and diverse populations. We shall not know the potential of unicameralism until some additional states decide to experiment.

Partisanship in Legislative Decision Making

VARIATIONS AMONG STATES

In some state legislatures the political party is the most important factor in decision making, and in some it has little or no significance; other legislatures are somewhere between these extremes. In most legislatures that normally have two parties substantially represented, the selection of legislative officers and committees is made along partisan lines. Such an organizational structure does not necessarily mean that either party is cohesive in voting on legislative issues, but it appears to be a prerequisite to higher levels of party activity.

There may be evidence of party cohesion at several stages of the legislative process. In the committees of some legislatures decisions are frequently made along party lines. In Pennsylvania, for example, most of the committee work is done by the chairman and a small core of majority party members, and the minority members of committees are usually unable to block majority ratification of the decisions reached by this small group. In some states, however, the critical legislative decisions are not made in committee. There is also great variety among two-party legislatures in the use of the caucus. In some states it has only an organizational function. In others, the leadership may call a meeting of the caucus in order to rally partisan support for a particularly important bill. Even if no binding votes are taken, the individual member is likely to be influenced by the caucus if there is evidence of consensus among the members on an issue. In a few states, such as Connecticut and New Jersey, the caucus assumes greater importance. In Connecticut, the caucus meets daily (often for a longer meeting than the legislative session), it debates most of the important bills that are on the legislative calendar, and it takes votes that—unless very close—are binding on the membership.

The preliminary party decision concerning a bill may be made in committee or in caucus, or it may be made informally by the party leaders after discussions with the governor, committee chairmen, or other interested members of the legislative party. A contested roll call on which at least one party is highly cohesive suggests that a decision has been reached, by one of these means, to take a party stand. Sometimes, however, high party cohesion is not the result of such preliminary decisions. The bill may simply have been sponsored by a highly respected member of one party (or a controversial member of the other), or it may have a similar impact on most of the constituencies represented by the members of one party.

There are a variety of methods for measuring party cohesion on roll-call votes. Because the legislature votes, and in some states takes roll calls, on a large number of noncontroversial bills, roll calls without much or any opposition (often with less than 10 per cent of the voting opposing the majority) are generally omitted from calculations. One rough measure of partisanship in legislative voting is the proportion of contested roll calls on which a majority of the two parties take opposite stands. It has been over 80 per cent in southern New England states, 40 to 65 per cent in several northern industrial states, and one-third or less in some other two-party states. Although we do not have roll-call data from all state legislatures and studies in various states have used different measuring guides, it is evident that the proportion of highly partisan roll calls varies greatly among the two-party legislatures. It is highest in some of the most industrialized and urban states of the northeast and midwest and lowest in some of the western states.

REQUISITES FOR LEGISLATIVE PARTISANSHIP

The members of a legislative party are most likely to vote in the same manner on frequent roll calls when they represent similar constituency interests. The legislatures in which a high proportion of Democratic and Republican members often vote on opposite sides are in states where each party represents a distinct and relatively homogeneous interest. In such states most Democratic legislators come from the large cities and represent particularly labor union members, lower-income workers, and ethnic and racial minorities. Republican legislators usually represent small towns, farm areas, and some suburban areas. The legislative strength of the parties is more concentrated geographically than their electoral strength because some of their votes are wasted under any districting system. This bipolarization is clearest in states where most of the Democratic legislators represent one or a few metropolitan centers, such as Michigan, and it is least likely to be found in the more rural states where the Democratic party must draw much of its legislative strength from outside the large cities.

In the states with bipolarized legislative parties, the images of two parties are likely to be distinctly different; the Democrats are the more liberal, and the Republicans the more conservative. These differences may be manifest in their platforms and in the promises and records of their state candidates and officeholders. It would be a mistake, however, to assume that most voters perceive the state parties in ideological terms or support a party because it is liberal or conservative. This assumption would contradict the findings of voting behavior studies over the last decade. As John Wahlke and his associates have shown in *The Legislative System,* it is even doubtful that the differences between the ideological beliefs of Democratic and Republican legislators are greater in states with high party cohesion than in those where party cohesion is relatively low.

The source of high party cohesion and clear differences between the two legislative parties is what Frank Sorauf calls in *Party and Representation* "an inarticulate ideology—the common interests and goals of the similar constituencies from which they draw their most loyal partisans."

If the members of a legislative party represent similar constituencies, the individual legislator is less likely to experience serious conflicts between the viewpoints of most of the legislators in his party and the views of dominant groups in his own constituency. He is free from conflicting pressures and he finds it easy to go along when his party takes a stand on a bill. In legislatures where the parties each represent homogeneous interests party regularity on roll calls is likely to be a legislative norm. The new legislator discovers that he is expected to support the party's position on bills unless to do so would cause serious difficulties within his constituency. The norm of party regularity may be reinforced by a variety of devices. The floor leaders or someone in the governor's office may talk to individual members, or caucuses may be held with varying degrees of frequency. In a few states with particularly strong party organizations, state party leaders may be able to use the local party as a device for putting pressure on the recalcitrant legislator. More often, the local party organizations approach legislators only with respect to issues that have some local impact.

Party leaders may apply pressure on the rank-and-file legislator through the use of well known rewards and sanctions: patronage, local projects, choice committee assignments, and support for—or opposition to—bills sponsored by the legislator. The potency of these incentives varies from state to state, but it is not difficult to find examples of each being used effectively by party leaders. Even in states where the use of such pressures is familiar, party regularity is likely to be more a custom or a norm than the consequence of pressure. The rewards are too scarce and the sanctions too disruptive to be used frequently. The purposes of caucuses and meetings with the party leadership are primarily those of communicating the party's position and reinforcing conformity to that position.

In those state legislatures where the party represents a wide diversity of constituency interests, there is no basis for high party cohesion. Party regularity is not broadly accepted as an important norm. The party leadership seldom tries to adopt a party position on a bill, and when it does the legislator discovers that he can vote against his party with impunity. If a caucus meets, its decisions are not binding and it may frequently adjourn in disunity. The rewards and sanctions at the disposal of the leadership are either too few or are ineffective. The administration party may support the governor if his prestige is at stake in a bill, but in most two-party states with weak legislative parties the governor is reluctant to risk his prestige by frequently committing it to legislative issues.

In those legislatures where party regularity is a widely accepted norm we should not expect to find two highly cohesive parties opposing each other on all or most roll calls. The legislative calendar is crowded with bills that affect only a few narrow interests or that have an effect only in one locality. Many of these measures are noncontroversial and lead to nearly unanimous roll calls; others cause some controversy but do not affect important interests to which either of the parties is committed. On other bills the parties may avoid taking a stand because interests that should not be alienated are arrayed on opposite sides of the issue. If partisan control of the legislature is divided, the groups supporting a bill may try to avoid its becoming a partisan measure in order to avoid a deadlock between the two houses. In a legislature with two strong, cohesive parties there are many reasons why a large proportion of bills do not become partisan issues. There are other bills on which the parties take conflicting positions that are not manifest in the roll calls because compromises are devised in committee or behind the scenes that make possible a nearly unanimous vote.

PARTISAN ISSUES

On the basis of roll-call studies in a number of states it is possible to distinguish three categories of bills that most often produce a high level of party cohesion: administration bills; those concerning broad social or economic issues; and, those involving the interests of the party or legislative organization. Although state administrative agencies may support a large number of bills, the governor usually is more cautious and takes a stand on a small proportion of them. The more strongly the governor becomes committed to a bill, the more likely the administration party is to unite in support of him and the greater the incentive for the opposition party to take a stand different from, if not completely contrary to, the governor's stand. Although roll-call studies have seldom identified precisely the bills on which governors were committed, they have shown that party cohesion is usually high on certain kinds of issues that almost automatically involve the governor's prestige. Examples of these are appropriations, taxation bills, gubernatorial appointments, and bills affecting state government administration. It is also likely that many important social and economic issues are part of the governor's program; these would provide an even greater likelihood of high party cohesion.

Many kinds of social and economic issues might produce high party cohesion. These would include labor legislation, the regulation of major business interests, and bills affecting the health, education, and welfare services provided by government. These issues are important to the legislative parties because they are important to the major interests that these parties represent. It is on such issues that the parties are likely to be committed, by their campaign promises and by their previous legislative records. Although the average voter may be unaware of this commitment and of the record made by the legislative party on these issues, the interest groups will be conscious of both. In the more urban states, where party cohesion is high, the differences between the parties regarding these issues are likely to be clear; they will tend to parallel the differences between the national Democratic and Republican parties.

The third category of issues includes those that primarily affect the party organization and usually have little importance for the public. As William J. Keefe has noted in his "Comparative Study of the Role of Political Parties in State Legislatures," the party's role in regard to these bills is that of a pressure group. At issue may be the administration of elections, the oversight of patronage, the transfer of appointing authority from one governmental official or unit to another, or the curtailment of power exercised by a political official. Equally bitter conflicts may develop over bills that would bolster the position of the majority party, embarrass officials in the minority party, or restrict the political opportunities available to both parties. Somewhat similar categories of measures are those that involve the interests of the legislative party: selection of the presiding officer; adoption and amendment of the rules; and certain procedural motions. Even in states where party cohesion is low, roll calls on matters of this kind are likely to produce high cohesion, although, as William Buchanan has demonstrated in California, a breakdown of party unity on such votes is a clear sign of a weak legislative party structure.

WHAT ARE THE ALTERNATIVES TO PARTISANSHIP?

In legislatures dominated by a single party or with weak or divided parties, we might expect some other groups, factions, or individual leaders to substitute for the party and to provide the legislator with voting cues on roll calls. It is well known that on specific bills certain legislators command a following because of their knowledge and experience concerning the issue. On other bills coalitions may form on some basis, such as geography, that the experienced observer can recognize. These are not substitutes for party leadership or organization because the leaders and coalitions shift from one issue to another. We are seeking to determine whether some pattern of continuity in legislative voting, or some legislative structure to take the place of the party, may exist.

In some one-party states, particularly in the South, the governor provides a continuing source of leadership. His support of, or opposition to, a bill makes a difference because a substantial proportion of legislators follow his lead. Such a governor cannot command the partisan loyalty of legislators, but he may obtain and hold their support simply because he is governor and has a specific legislative program to offer. In some southern legislatures, particularly during the first session of a governor's term, there seems to be a legislative norm that dictates at least sympathetic attention to the governor's legislative program. In addition, the governor of a one-party state has available, in varying quantities, the patronage and local projects utilized by the governor in a strong two-party state. The most significant advantage enjoyed by a governor in a one-party state is the absence of an opposition party. There is no legislative group that has the continuing responsibility for opposing or criticizing the governor's program, nor is there any opposition group in the legislature that has an organizational structure. The governor often has a floor leader; the opposition does not. Opposition groups that may form from time to time have no continuity. The patronage and other favors that a governor may dispense have a potential influence on any and all legislators in a one-party state. By contrast, legislators belonging to a strong opposition party are more likely to rebuff any gubernatorial offers in the expectation of benefitting when their party wins the governorship. Duane Lockard's description in *New England State Politics* of the New Hampshire governor as operating "in a power vacuum" is appropriate for most of the southern governors, who have usually enjoyed a high batting average in winning legislative approval for their programs.

In most of the southern states that have customarily had a strong governor, the constitution bars a second successive term for the chief executive officer and he is usually unable to pick his successor. Consequently, gubernatorial factions are seldom found in the legislature, and if they do develop during the term of one governor, they generally disappear when his successor takes office. Although there may be a group of legislators who are particularly loyal to the governor, an opposition faction is less likely to develop, particularly during the first session, because of the governor's political strength. The only clear example of gubernatorial factions in a southern legislature having continuity over a prolonged period has been in Louisiana, where Huey Long left a legacy of bifactionalism that has only recently begun to weaken.

There are other examples of factional patterns that occasionally emerge from legislative studies. There are liberal and conservative caucuses in the nonpartisan Minnesota legislature, but they have strong partisan roots. Buchanan's study of the California legislature in *Legislative Partisanship* demonstrated that for a while factions were more important than parties in determining voting patterns. In one-party and weak two-party states legislative leaders, such as the speaker and the chairmen of committees, may serve as effective leaders of cliques or factions. Florida and Texas are two states in which the pattern of roll-call voting appears to have a base in such factionalism. In some legislatures that are tightly controlled by a small group of leaders, however, the effects of such control are less evident in the roll calls. If the leadership is conservative, it may concentrate its efforts on blocking legislation in committee and may avoid floor action on the most controversial issues. In some legislatures a few strong leaders may limit their attention to a few pieces of legislation and may not seek to extend the span of their influence to a large enough number of bills to make their control visible in roll-call analyses.

Where there are neither two strong parties nor a strong governor, the most common result is simply a political vacuum. Coalitions formed one day disappear the next when a new bill reaches the floor of the legislature. There is greater opportunity for interest groups to exercise influence, and the changing patterns in the vote result in part from the changing balance of influence among lobbyists. The conclusion that Samuel C. Patterson drew from a careful search for voting patterns in the Oklahoma legislature would probably be accurate for many such states: "In the absence of party as a reference group, the legislator is likely, consciously or unconsciously, to respond to different pressures in different voting areas."

ARE PARTIES ESSENTIAL TO THE LEGISLATURE?

It is obvious that the legislature can operate, as it has in many states, with ineffective or nonexistent parties. On many of the technical and trivial issues that are of little concern to the public or concern only a few interests, there is little that the parties can or do contribute to the legislative decision-making process. The advocates of legislative partisanship do not argue that the legislature cannot operate without parties but that it cannot be *responsible* without parties.

From the viewpoint of the average voter, the legislative process is complex and confusing. The route that a bill must follow to passage is so tortuous that even the attentive citizen may lose track of it along the way. There are so many points at which critical decisions are made, sometimes behind the scenes, that even the best informed voter may be unable to determine who was responsible for blocking or amending a bill that interested him. In many states there is less information in the various news media about the state legislature than there is about Congress, and the record and statements of most legislators receive less attention from the media than that given to the average member of Congress. To be well informed about the record of the legislature and his legislator, a conscientious citizen must expend a prodigious amount of time and effort. In fact, the average voter is woefully ignorant about the state legislature. He does not often know what important bills are being considered or have been passed, and the subtle complexities of the legislative process are beyond his understanding and interest. Polls show that the average voter knows little or nothing about the voting record or public stands of his congressman, and it is probable that the voter's ignorance about his legislator's record is even greater—if that is possible.

If the average voter, or even the above-average voter, is to learn enough about the legislature to make an informed voting decision, he needs help —and the political party can provide that help. It is much easier for the voter to become familiar with the general record of the party in the legislature, and in the governor's office, than it is to become informed about the record of an individual legislator. If the voter is generally satisfied with what state government is doing, he can vote for the administration party; if dissatisfied, he can vote for a change in party. The legislative party can be responsible to the voters in a more meaningful sense than most individual legislators can be. The existence of parties simplifies the voter's task of understanding the legislative process, and if the result is sometimes oversimplification, this is preferable to confusion. These functions of the party are performed poorly or not at all by legislative factions—even in states where factions have some continuity and significance. "Factions that form and reform cannot become so identified in the minds of the electorate," as V. O. Key, Jr. noted in *Southern Politics*. Buchanan compared the factions in the California legislature to "bottles bearing no labels at all, but with somewhat different contents." The voter who cannot analyze the contents but is searching for a familiar label is lost.

If one argues that political parties can make the legislature more responsible to the voter, it must be admitted that the parties usually fall short of the classical standards of responsibility. Parties seldom campaign on a specific legislative program, legislative candidates are more interested in shaking hands than in clarifying issues, and the voter is only dimly aware of the issues discussed in the campaign. The average voter is more likely to recognize that a party represents certain interests and to turn against that party if he feels that these interests have been neglected. We have said that party cohesion is dependent on a homogeneity of interests represented by the party, what Sorauf describes as an "inarticulate ideology," and we would agree with him that this provides no more and no less than "a reasonable substitute for party responsibility."

In a state without a strong party system the governor may be deemed responsible to the voters if he campaigns on a platform and tries to win legislative enactment of his program. But, if he can neither serve a second term nor pick his successor, the voters have no opportunity to pass judgment on him. Moreover, legislative candidates in a one-party state rarely campaign with promises to support or oppose the governor's programs and consequently the voters have no means of electing legislators who can be counted on to cooperate with or to oppose the governor, and the records of individual legislators are usually not well enough known to help the voter make his decisions. Although it is true that some southern governors are able to carry out their campaign pledges to the voters because the legislature is compliant, voters in such states are unable to select a legislature that will act as a restraint on the governor or to select legislators who will form an opposition party. In the absence of a two-party system the governor may be thought responsible to the voters, but the legislature is much less likely to be.

Critics of legislative partisanship argue that strong parties may be detrimental to legislative responsibility in either of two ways. If different parties have majorities in the two houses or different parties control the legislature and governorship, the consequence of highly cohesive parties is likely to be deadlock. The voter is unable to pin responsibility for the defeat of legislation on either party. In a sense, the fragmentation of partisan control guarantees an element of irresponsibility in the legislative process. Reapportionment on the basis of population will eliminate one of the causes of divided government. On the other hand, divided government may increase as party competition grows and in some states a minority party becomes able to elect a governor before it is strong enough to win a legislative majority in both houses. The familiar constitutional practice of staggered legislative terms also makes divided government more likely. Concurrent four-year terms for the governor and all members of both houses are the constitutional prescription most likely to avoid divisions in the partisan control of government.

Strong legislative parties are also criticized because they may be so strong that the rank-and-file legislators become simply puppets, manipulated by the governor and the leaders of the party in the legislature or in the county. The legislator who has become a puppet, it is argued, is neglecting his responsibility to his constituents. Political scientists have long debated whether legislative parties should be responsible to the voters, in the sense of carrying out the programs that were campaign promises, or whether each legislator should make his own judgment about the wishes of his constituents, at the risk of causing paralyzing disunity in the party. In practice, as we have seen, parties are usually cohesive only where the legislators in each party represent similar districts, and consequently legislators face few conflicts between party and constituent demands. A more specific point is the charge that big-city political machines, often as a reward for faithful service, nominate legislators who are simply party hacks and who lack the ability to do more than follow instructions.

The population trend to the suburbs and the decline of urban machines are trends that may alleviate this problem but, in a larger sense, it is part of the continuing problem of recruiting more able men to legislative service. There is no reason why the growth of partisanship should be an obstacle to making legislative service more attractive and challenging.

Duane Lockard

4

The State Legislator

Any sound assessment of the state legislature must include more than the constitutional and procedural aspects of the institution; it must also consider the perspectives of individual members. Until recently, most writing on state legislatures seldom analyzed the attitudes, self-perceptions, and individual roles of members. Rather, the focus was on broad institutional features: constitutional provisions, legislative procedure, party organization, and the like. Many recent discussions of state legislative activity have likewise ignored the individual's role and have instead sought to explain legislative output through examination of variations in the social and economic characteristics of states. While all these approaches have utility, there is serious risk of failing to grasp the essence of a legislature if the perspective of the individual member is ignored.

A legislature is composed of individuals, and only by considering their attitudes, conceptions, and aspirations are we likely to answer satisfactorily the elusive riddle of why state legislatures vary so greatly from one state to another in their functioning and legislative output. Sophisticated correlations of state socio-economic factors (*e.g.*, income and education) with public policies in a number of areas have demonstrated that much of the variation in state legislative output can be explained by social and economic variations in the states. It has been shown also that, to a lesser degree, party competition relates to policy variations among states. But this leaves us short of a full explanation because the research is necessarily partial; it considers important facets of state politics but does not sufficiently explain remaining variations.

DUANE LOCKARD, *a former Connecticut State Senator, is Professor of Politics at Princeton University and Director of the Undergraduate Program of the Woodrow Wilson School. Professor Lockard's publications include* New England State Politics, The Connecticut Challenge Primary: A Study in Legislative Power, *and* The Politics of State and Local Government.

98

To assess the distinct political traditions and practices of states and the related behavior patterns of state legislatures is admittedly not a simple undertaking. Adequate monographic studies of politics in at least half the states do not exist. But for states that have been analyzed, a more adequate understanding is possible than purely quantitative research provides.

In short, there is every reason to believe that the existing political ethos of a state conditions the way a legislature functions as well as its legislative output. Those who enter the legislature have their attitudes and expectations shaped in part by that ethos. The relative importance of political parties, for example, deeply affects the expectations of a new legislator. If the party system is weak and the tradition of political independence is strong, obviously this fact will have an impact on the conduct of legislative business. If the political ethos leads a legislator to feel that his proper role is to decide each question for himself without bowing to the will of a strong party leadership clique, manifestly this will produce a different legislative atmosphere than a political system which induces the new member to accept party discipline as a matter of course. Because the legislature is a human institution, the beliefs that its members acquire within it are important determinants of how it functions and what it produces.

Legislators' Self-perceptions

Two recent pieces of scholarship illustrate the possibilities for investigation of the individual member's attitudes as an important aspect of legislative behavior. John C. Wahlke, Heinz Eulau, William Buchanan, and LeRoy C. Ferguson studied the self-perceptions of legislators from California, New Jersey, Ohio, and Tennessee and reported their findings in *The Legislative System*. They demonstrated that considerable variation in role perception—how the legislator views his own part in the legislative process—occurs among legislators within and among these four states. They categorized legislators in different respects—as to their perception of their role as a representative, their approach to interest groups, and their sense of whether they are primarily district or state oriented. They found, for example, that three times as many Ohio legislators saw themselves as "brokers," dealing with the conflicting demands of diverse interests, than were found in the Tennessee legislature. Similarly, three times as many Ohio members saw themselves playing a dual role as both broker and "inventor" (in the sense of an initiator of policy) than in Tennessee.

Some legislators, Wahlke, *et al.*, contend, come to office with what is called a "trustee" conception of their role; that is, they think of themselves as free agents who should make up their minds as to their own judgment of issues—more or less in the classic style of Burke's "Speech to the Electors of Bristol." The trustee does not trust lobbyists, leaders, or colleagues, and thinks of himself as one who acts on principles rather than political pressures. The "delegate," on the other hand, feels he should reflect the will of his constituents, more or less in majoritarian fashion, even if his constituents want something that he disagrees with. The "politico," however, shares some of each of these beliefs. One holding this role-orientation tends to be "more sensitive to conflicting alternatives, more flexible in the ways in which he tries to resolve the conflict among alternatives, and less dogmatic in his orientation toward legislative behavior as it is related to his representational role."

Roughly a quarter of the California, New Jersey, and Ohio legislators were classified as politicos, but only 13 per cent of Tennessee's legislators were in this category. Significantly, four out of five Tennessee legislators believed their proper role to be that of trustee. The highest proportion of state legislators in the delegate category was in California, and the lowest in Tennessee. This reflects prevailing myths in the specific states more than hard reality, for the history of California legislative politics does not suggest that any unusually effective reflection of constituent views prevails there. William Buchanan points out in his study of California legislative development, *Legislative Partisanship,* that the progressive doctrines of Hiram Johnson struck deep roots in California politics, and no doubt the high incidence of delegate role-orientation is related to the Progressive ethos.

Many legislators who profess to subscribe to one or another of these role-orientations will in practice not conform to it, or may rationalize their behavior to fit under the rubric even if the rationalization is far-fetched. I have known many legislators who expressed convictions that would make them "delegates" and who always find some excuse for their behavior in constituency opinion, however flimsy the evidence may be.

Although such rationalization takes place, it does not follow that the attitudes of legislators are irrelevant for legislative behavior. That a member articulates a particular philosophy regarding the proper style of representation may not mean that he will uniformly adhere to the doctrine, but it certainly affects the manner in which he relates to other actors in the political arena. If he is basically suspicious of interest groups and deeply committed to weighing all aspects of an issue in terms of his personal principles, the opportunity to influence him will accordingly be less than if he held either a delegate or politico orientation. Some support for this general position is to be found in Oliver Garceau and Corinne Silverman's analysis of the Vermont legislature, "A Pressure Group and the Pressured," where they found many legislators who professed essentially the trustee position, although they did not so identify it. Because of the suspicious attitude of many rural Republican legislators toward big business lobbyists, as well as longstanding hostile Farm Bureau attitudes, the representatives of the Associated Industries of Vermont did not try to make mass appeals to the legislative membership, but worked instead through a few selected leaders.

LIMITATIONS IN ROLE-ORIENTED ANALYSES

Significant although role-orientations may be for affecting the behavior of legislators, the limitations of this approach to the comprehension of a legislature must be recognized. In the first place, the degree of commitment to a role may be limited. If deeply held, the sense of proper role may greatly affect behavior, but at times practice conflicts strongly with belief. Furthermore, reliance on role categories as a means to comprehension of the legislature is complicated by the fact that a legislator may fit into different categories under different circumstances, or when viewed by observers with different perspectives in the course of their classification of legislators in interviews. Wahlke, *et al.*, encounter this problem when they classify legislators in terms of their attitude toward interest-group pressures. Their categories are "facilitator," "neutral," and "resister," and the meanings of the terms are exactly what the titles suggest. The facilitator knows much about interest-group activity and is receptive to it. The resister also knows much about the activity, but is hostile toward it. And the neutrals have no strong feelings about interest-group activity regardless of their knowledge of it.

As one would expect, the lowest level of resisters in any of the four states was found in California, where some of the most flamboyant lobbying operations in history have taken place. Almost equally expected, the highest proportions of facilitators were found in the two states with the strongest partisan influence, New Jersey and Ohio. However, the analytic value of this finding is limited by the inevitable tendency for the legislators to have different attitudes about different interest groups. Vermont farmers might take a strong position about the dangers of falling prey to interest groups and castigate big business lobbyists in strong language, while at the same time being highly receptive to the appeals of representatives of the American Farm Bureau Federation.

THE LAWMAKER

In *The Lawmakers*, James David Barber may be less subject to criticism in his classification than some others because he is primarily concerned with the psychological orientation of the individual rather than the profession of principles of behavior. Barber's is not a comparative analysis since it deals with Connecticut alone, but he poses some highly significant questions about the kind of person who becomes a legislator. He identifies four types: the "spectator," the "advertiser," the "reluctant," and the "lawmaker." The spectator is more entertained by than a contributor to the legislative arena, a person who is awed by the pomp and ceremony of legislative life and the opportunity to rub elbows with celebrities. Said one of a governor's tea for legislators: "We were very impressed. I mean you couldn't help but be impressed. . . . The Governor and his wife met us graciously and gave us the full roam of the house—'Go ahead, look at anything you want. Make yourself at home. . . .' " Especially sensitive to approval and disapproval, insecure, and other-directed, the spectator is a common type of state legislator, but not one who makes a significant contribution to the process.

The advertiser is also a common type of legislative flower: he is a legislator because he wishes to advertise himself—"ethically"—for his future career, legal or other. He is more active than the spectator and has more training and ability, but his ambition is not primarily political, and his role in the legislature is more frustrating than satisfying. He has a sense of impotence and high self-consciousness of what he deems to be his sacrifices and the abuse of him by others.

The reluctant, like the spectator, is not very active in the legislature, and is usually retired, bewildered by the alien world of the legislature, and he feels sometimes pitifully inadequate to perform tasks that he cannot even comprehend. Often recruited because he bears a proud family name that will garner votes, or because of long civic activity in a small community that wins him a wide circle of friends, he comes to the legislature ill equipped for the combat and confusion he finds there. He is a carrier of traditional values and perhaps his major contribution to the legislative process is his sense of decorum and his desire to suppress open conflict.

In contrast with the other types, the lawmaker is a strong personality: confident, capable, and deeply involved in the substantive aspects of legislative work. He is interested in issues, capable of working with others to achieve results, and has a high potential and ambition for political advancement. Barber found that a little over a third of his sample of first-term members of the lower house of the Connecticut General Assembly fell into the lawmaker category, and he believes that any future significant role for state legislatures will depend in part upon the capacity of the political system to identify and recruit more lawmaker types. For the identification of the lawmaker Barber stresses certain criteria: the extent to which individuals have thrown themselves into the work of organizations to which they belong, their persistence in the organizing activities of the groups in which they participate, evidence of emphasis on political issues broadly defined, occupational security, and evidence—so far as ascertainable—of personal self-confidence and security.

Recruiting more lawmaker types is no simple process, and throwing the rascals out, in the shopworn phrase of reformism, is not enough. Excellence does not automatically replace the shoddy. Reforms like the raising of legislative salaries, the provision of staff assistance, and lengthening sessions will not, by themselves, necessarily improve the quality of candidates. More conscientious efforts by those who recruit legislative candidates is also indispensable if the state legislature is not to sink still further in prestige and significance in the American scheme of government.

The Amateur Legislator

One reason why sheer competence for the legislative task is so important is that so many state legislators are rank novices. From observation I feel confident that even those who lack formal training in the law or in the intricacies of policy making can nevertheless make significant contributions as legislators if they stay in office a few terms. Some of the most effective legislators I know have never had formal education beyond high school, but their knowledge of their field of policy specialization is impressive and their capacity for dealing with other actors in the legislative arena is enormous. Such individuals begin their legislative careers as relatively worthless members for the simple reason that unfamiliarity with the legislative world prevents them from realizing their potential at an early stage.

HIGH TURNOVER

Unfortunately, the average state legislature has a very high proportion of first-term members; turnover is very rapid in most states. Table 1 sets forth the percentages of first-term members in each state as of 1963. (That year was chosen because neither the 1960 nor the 1962 elections were landslides that would have swept in unusually high percentages of newcomers.) Just over one-third of all legislators are newcomers, a percentage that apparently has not varied greatly during the last few decades. Charles S. Hyneman analyzed the "Tenure and Turnover of Legislative Personnel" in ten state legislatures during the period 1925-35 and found the average percentage of newcomers for lower houses to be 40 per cent and upper houses 20 per cent. A somewhat higher figure was reported in *American State Legislatures* for the year 1950 by a committee of the American Political Science Association; in that study the composite percentage of first-term members for both houses was 42 per cent.

The tenure of upper house membership tends to be longer than for lower houses. The median percentage of first-term members in the forty-nine upper houses in 1963 (omitting Nebraska's unicameral body) was 28 per cent, while for lower houses it was 38 per cent. The problem of amateurism may be somewhat mitigated in reality for senates, since an unknown number of first-term members there have graduated from the lower chamber. However, detailed information on that point for all states is difficult to gather.

EXPLAINING HIGH TURNOVER

There appears to be no way to predict from general data on state political systems whether the level of turnover will be high or low. Neither

Table 1: First-Term Membership in State Legislatures.

State	Upper House Members			Lower House Members		
	New	Total	% New	New	Total	% New
Alabama	28	35	80%	63	106	59%
Alaska	7	20	35%	17	40	43%
Arizona	7	28	25%	35	80	44%
Arkansas	13	35	37%	29	100	29%
California	11	40	28%	39	80	49%
Colorado	7	35	20%	23	65	35%
Connecticut	10	36	28%	105	294	36%
Delaware	4	17	24%	14	35	40%
Florida	10	38	26%	29	95	31%
Georgia	48	54	89%	84	205	41%
Hawaii	10	25	40%	13	51	25%
Idaho	15	44	34%	23	63	37%
Illinois	11	58	19%	38	177	21%
Indiana	13	50	26%	41	100	41%
Iowa	16	50	32%	24	108	22%
Kansas	5	40	13%	34	125	27%
Kentucky	13	38	34%	67	100	67%
Louisiana	4	39	10%	5	105	5%
Maine	13	33	39%	78	151	52%
Maryland	14	29	48%	81	142	57%
Massachusetts	12	40	30%	55	240	23%
Michigan	11	34	32%	24	110	22%
Minnesota	23	67	34%	57	135	42%
Mississippi	2	49	4%	7	140	5%
Missouri	6	33	18%	61	163	37%
Montana	11	56	20%	42	94	45%
Nebraska		15/43	35% (combined)			
Nevada	5	17	29%	12	37	32%
New Hampshire	13	24	54%	155	400	39%
New Jersey	3	21	14%	26	60	43%
New Mexico	0	32	0%	28	66	46%
New York	9	58	16%	27	150	18%
North Carolina	33	50	66%	52	120	43%
North Dakota	14	49	29%	38	113	34%
Ohio	9	33	27%	35	137	26%
Oklahoma	10	44	23%	42	120	35%
Oregon	10	30	33%	25	60	42%
Pennsylvania	11	50	22%	46	210	22%
Rhode Island	18	46	39%	30	100	30%
South Carolina	12	46	26%	47	124	38%
South Dakota	14	35	40%	30	75	22%
Tennessee	18	33	54%	57	99	58%
Texas	12	31	39%	67	150	45%
Utah	9	25	36%	39	64	61%
Vermont	11	30	37%	98	246	40%
Virginia	2	40	5%	21	100	21%
Washington	9	49	18%	26	99	26%
West Virginia	6	32	19%	44	100	44%
Wisconsin	8	33	24%	21	100	21%
Wyoming	7	27	26%	15	56	27%
TOTALS*	615	1831	34%	2006	5834	34%

* Not inclusive of Nebraska. Totals for *all* state legislators of both houses, including Nebraska, are 2636/7708, or 34%.

Source: Council of State Governments, Book of the States, *1963-64.*

the extent of party competition, the size of houses, nor legislative salary levels is an index of turnover, as Tables 2, 3, and 4 indicate. Note that

Table 2: *Percentage of First-Term Members by Size of Lower Houses in 1963.*

	High*	Medium	Low
100 members or larger	11	7	13
under 100 members	10	4	4

* High percentages: 40 and above; Medium: 30-39; Low: under 30.
Source: Council of State Governments, Book of the States, *1964-65.*

Table 3: *Percentage of First-Term Members of Lower Houses**
Compared with Legislative Salaries.

Percentage of First-Term Members	Salaries†			
	Low	Medium	High	
High‡	9	8	3	20
Medium	5	4	1	10
Low	10	2	8	20
TOTALS	24	14	12	

* Includes Nebraska's unicameral legislature.
† Omits expense allowances, since they cannot be accurately estimated for many states.
‡ High percentages: 40 and above; Medium: 30-39; Low: under 30.
Source: Council of State Governments, Book of the States, *1964-65.*

two-party states tend to have fairly high proportions of first-term members; the same, however, is true of noncompetitive states. Likewise, size of membership has little direct correlation with turnover. There is a slight correlation between legislative salaries and tenure, but not the strong relationship that is often implied by the contention that low salaries are the chief reason for high turnover. It is significant that nine states with high turnover also have low salaries, and that eight with high salaries have low turnover, but the random scattering of most states indicates that the relationship between salaries and tenure is certainly not a decisive factor.

Whether turnover is high or low obviously depends upon political conditions within the state. Some states throughout the period for which data are available have had very low turnover (*e.g.,* Illinois, Louisiana, Mississippi, and New York), while others have had consistently high turnover (*e.g.,* Alabama, Indiana, Maine, and Oregon). Given the stark contrasts in the politics of these states, it is difficult to generalize on the causes of short tenure. In some cases the turnover is imposed by a tradition that different parts of a district will be represented in successive elections

Table 4: Percentage of First-Term Members in Lower Houses of Legislatures as of 1963, by Degree of Party Competition. *

	High (over 40%)	Medium (30-39%)	Low (under 30%)
Two-Party States	9	7	11
One-Party Dominant States	5	1	2
One-Party States	5	2	4

* These are the classifications used by Malcolm Jewell in Chapter 3 of this volume.
Source: Council of State Governments, Book of the States, *1964-65.*

in a rotational system, but this probably is not the prime cause of high turnover since in many states with high turnover no such tradition prevails.

Some slight mitigation of the disadvantage of amateurism may be found in intensive orientation sessions for new members. Some states now attempt to introduce new members to the legislative process through such training programs. To a degree, this may assist newcomers in learning the strange language and mysterious procedures of the legislature, but even an ambitious educational undertaking of this kind will not greatly affect the problems of amateurism. For the difficulty of the amateur is not just that the language and procedures are unfamiliar; he is at a disadvantage because he is not familiar with the political morés of the legislature and simply has not been around long enough to feel sufficiently confident to assert himself. No training session can provide what experience teaches by a slow pedagogy.

Occupational and Social Background of Legislators

Whatever their deficiencies, the bulk of state legislators have a better education and higher social standing than the constituencies that elect them. As William J. Keefe has noted in *The American Legislative Process,* "The typical legislator is far from a typical citizen. Not only is his career launched from a more elevated social station than the typical citizen's, but it is also launched amid more of the social advantages conferred by education." Keefe also reports that between two-thirds and three-fourths of the members of the Illinois, Indiana, Iowa, and Missouri legislatures had attended college, and that a majority of the 1961 Indiana legislature were college graduates. The 1949 occupational distribution of all state legislators reported in *American State Legislatures* showed that 22 per cent were lawyers, 23 per cent were engaged in business, and 4 per cent were physicians and teachers. The decline of agriculture as a source of employment and the impact of reapportionment on rural over-representation have reduced the proportion of farmers in legislatures since the 1949 tabulation, when 20 per cent of legislators were farmers.

It is sometimes said, however, that the professionals and businessmen who go into the legislature are second-raters, men who would not take up politics if they were successful in their careers. This kind of sweeping judgment is difficult to controvert, but at least where criteria for measurement exist—as to some extent it does for lawyers—the evidence belies the canard. In "The Lawyer as Decision-Maker in the American State Legislature," David R. Derge reported a painstaking survey of lawyers in the Illinois and Missouri legislatures. He found, by checking with the standard rating of lawyers by Martindale-Hubbell, that lawyer-legislators "were on the whole at least as good as, and sometimes superior to, their professional colleagues outside the assembly halls."

Legislators as an "In-group"

Once a session of a state legislature is well under way, an "in-group" feeling begins to develop. Pressures from lobbyists, constituents, party or factional leaders, and the governor induce a fellowship of common cause that transcends party or factional lines. Newcomers, being so numerous, are not frozen out to the extent that freshmen in the United States Congress are, and the membership as a whole relatively soon acquires a sense of shared experiences. The common interest in politics provides a basis for making acquaintances easily; and since politicians tend to be more than normally out-going personalities, there is much socializing both during and after session hours. The state capitol is often remote enough from the representative's home to make commuting impossible, and the costs and inconvenience of moving families thus means that the state capital's hotels are the gathering place for temporary bachelor-legislators who, being thrown together and not preoccupied by family, spend more time socializing than they would at home. Hotel bars and lobbies, during after-hours, teem with legislators and lobbyists swapping gossip and reminiscing about political exploits.

THE CLUB ATMOSPHERE

Still, the sense of the state legislature as a "club" is not nearly as strong as, for example, it is with the Congress and especially the United States Senate. Short terms, brief tenure, and the amateurism of the state legislature work against the development of intense loyalty to the legislative group that prevails in Congress. There is, however, much of the same decorousness of formal language on the floor. Such indeed is almost a necessity to prevent the underlying current of conflict from making life miserable for all members. Furthermore, legislators soon become aware that today's antagonist may be tomorrow's ally, someone whom the member must not only get along with socially, but also politically. Thus, it is not uncommon to see sharp conflict in a caucus or committee room or on the floor of the legislature between two members who, when the issue is settled, will socialize together.

DEFERENCE TO COLLEAGUES

Deference to the wishes of colleagues often is carried to quite extreme lengths. Although in only a few states does the rule of "senatorial courtesy," as it prevails in the United States Senate, permit the rejection of a chief executive's nominee because a member finds the nominee "personally objectionable," lesser variants on that rule are common. Members are often permitted by tradition to defer a vote either in committee or on the floor until they can muster all possible opposition or support. In Massachusetts, for example, a neophyte learned a tradition that he never knew existed when an older member moved to table a bill. The newcomer rose to ask the President of the Senate if he could later move to take the bill off the table if he voted to table in the first instance. He was told that he could but, after the vote was cast, an oldtimer leaned over and told him that not for two hundred years had anybody been so presumptuous as to move to take from the table what another Massachusetts senator had put there. The new member did not break decorum and went along with tradition.

THE PRESS AND THE LEGISLATOR

A significant aspect of the in-group feeling is the relationship that often prevails between members of the press and the legislators. Each side needs the other's cooperation—the reporter needs news and the legislator needs (or at least enjoys) publicity—but often there is considerable tension between the two, since to some extent they work at cross purposes. The legislator may want desperately to keep some kinds of news from reporters—whether legitimately or illegitimately—and the reporter wants all the information he can get.

Reporters around state legislatures are often cynical and highly critical, and legislators, sometimes quite justifiably, become annoyed at the holier-than-thou sermons that reporters and columnists preach through their newspapers. The result is an ambiguous set of relationships—mutual suspicion and mutual dependence—producing such tension that an open battle may break out, as it did in Tennessee a few years ago when the legislature barred the reporters of a specific newspaper from the legislative halls. (A court order readmitted them.) This is an extreme case, to be sure, but the problem it illustrates is genuine. There is enough dereliction of duty in legislative halls to merit criticism, but sometimes the criticism is so destructive and unfair that it not only produces resentment but greatly contributes to an unfavorable public image of the legislature.

The Recruitment and Election of Legislators

The manner of recruiting legislators varies widely from one political system to another. In some situations the aspiring candidate generates his own independent campaign, while in other cases, party or factional leaders either screen potential aspirants or actively recruit among those who have not specifically offered themselves as candidates. The former situation—self-recruitment—is most likely to occur where party organization is weak, as in some predominantly one-party areas, or where a tradition of wide-open primaries prevails. In such areas the party leaders make no effort to select or endorse candidates, waiting until the primaries have been held before involving themselves at all. One result of this inactivity may be that no nominees come forth and that the electorate is denied any choice at all.

The minority party often puts up no candidates in legislative districts dominated by one party. In some states, as many as 50 to 60 per cent of the districts will have only one candidate on the ballot. Nor is this practice limited to the extreme one party states. In New Hampshire, for example, 59 per cent of the seats for the House of Representatives were uncontested in 1950. While California operated on the cross-filing system (whereby a candidate could file in both party primaries without identifying his own party affiliation), there were many uncontested elections. In Illinois, Kentucky, and Missouri there is a tendency for candidacies not to be filled. In Illinois, this is apparently the result of the cumulative voting system that encourages deals between party leaders to split the three-member districts on a two-and-one basis in noncompetitive areas, thus eliminating the necessity to compete in campaigns.

In many other states virtually every possible candidacy is filled. In Connecticut, New Jersey, and New York, for example, nearly 100 per cent of all candidacies are filled, however hopeless the prospect may be in one-sided districts. This situation may change as state party organizations from time to time wax and wane. In Maine, during the long period when the Democratic party was moribund, only about half of all seats were contested, but more recently four out of five seats are subject to competition. Over longer periods of time, in the judgment of the late V. O. Key, Jr., expressed in *American State Politics,* the primary election system has so weakened the party organization that local organizations are unable or unwilling to make the effort to fill candidacies. To test his point, he selected two states in which the primary has had little or no impact (Connecticut and Indiana) and two in which the primary became fully operative (Missouri and Ohio) and compared them as to the proportions of uncontested legislative seats. Between 1908 and 1948 the Connecticut and Indiana proportions of uncontested seats increased only insignificantly, while in Missouri and Ohio the proportions rose dramatically (from 1-2 per cent to 20-30).

RECRUITMENT OF LEGISLATORS

Active recruitment and/or control over nominations by party organizations has several consequences for the legislative aspirant. In some cases active recruitment brings to the fore potentially able legislators who otherwise might never have been considered, and it may close out some aspirants (both fit and unfit) whom the organization expects either not to win or not to be "trustworthy" from the organization's point of view. Whether on balance one is inclined to believe that organizational recruitment will improve or worsen the quality of legislators depends upon one's attitude toward party organization. (On this subject there is an absence of both data and standards for evaluating such information that might be collected. Undoubtedly, active recruitment does at times turn up highly competent legislators who can be persuaded by assurances of support to run in the primary and general elections. In my own opinion the potential improvement that could follow from more active recruitment by party leaders would be great if it were done conscientiously and with an eye to the qualities that a good legislator must possess.

Where recruitment is aimed at merely filling a candidacy by a name, without regard to potential contribution in the legislature, the results may be more negative than positive. By this route we get what Barber calls the "reluctants," those who were persuaded to enter the race but have few qualifications for office. In the sample he used (the 1959 lower house in Connecticut) there probably was an unusually high proportion of such reluctants, since in Connecticut almost all legislative seats are contested and the 1958 election resulted in a landslide that brought into office a great number of representatives who never even remotely expected to be elected. This created a severe problem for the Democrats, with a margin of two seats, in maintaining their majority for vital legislative votes, particularly because many surprised victors found it difficult to get to the capital regularly. Furthermore, it filled legislative ranks with some individuals little qualified for the task.

Party organizations are not, however, the only sources for recruitment. Interest groups, campaign contributors, and fund solicitors also attempt to promote candidacies from time to time. This is probably far less common than party recruitment and tends to occur most often where party control over nominations is weakest. Interest-group recruitment may not produce lawmakers in the sense in which that word is used here, but in some cases contributor recruitment effort may advance lawmaker types who might not otherwise present themselves.

WINNING RECOGNITION AS A CANDIDATE

From the point of view of the candidate for the legislature, one of the most difficult aspects of the campaign is winning recognition in his constituency. His campaign efforts, particularly in a presidential election year, are likely to be obscured by the all-encompassing attention devoted to the candidates in the center ring. It is difficult to avoid being swept along with the tide, regardless of the effort put into a campaign, especially in an election like that of 1964 when many able Republican legislators were swept aside, not because of their own shortcomings but because of Barry Goldwater's unpopularity. The reverse of this is illustrated by the story told about a Democratic candidate for the state legislature from New York City in 1936. The worried candidate kept badgering his district party leader to help him with his campaign, saying that he was getting no publicity and was scared. The leader asked the candidate if he had ever seen the Staten Island Ferry dock. "Notice that when it comes in," he said, "it brings a lot of garbage in with it. The garbage never brings in the ferry; it's the ferry that sweeps in the garbage. Roosevelt is your ferry, boy, so don't worry."

Conditions are rarely that simple. The candidate has to find a way of winning some recognition in his constituency, a task complicated by lack of campaign funds and by the low level of general interest in state legislative affairs. When I ran for state senator in Connecticut I met hundreds of people who scarcely knew for what I was running and cared less. This was impressed upon me by an incident at a cocktail party a few months after I won the election. I met a man who, when introduced to me, said sure, he knew me, had met me during the campaign and had voted for me. I thanked him politely but was grateful that the noise of the cocktail party allowed me to be noncommittal about his next question, which was, "Well, now that you're elected, how are things down in Washington?"

CAMPAIGNING IS CONFUSION

Campaigning for office is somewhat like fighting in a dark room; you never know fully what the strategic situation is, what the opposition is accomplishing, whether your own efforts are doing any good. This is particularly true of legislative candidacies, since the candidate himself must likely attend to all campaign details without the help of staff members available to candidates for higher office. While trying to pursue an occupation to support his family, he must go to all possible meetings, arrange the taping of radio broadcasts, persuade the printer to extend further credit, write press releases, keep up the morale of whatever volunteer stamp-lickers are around, and on and on. Of course, there are enormous variations from area to area in the conduct of campaigns. In one-party areas in some small districts the candidate may spend almost no money and put little effort into his campaign; in other places the candidate may have to cover a wide area and feel that his only chance is by leaving nothing undone that might squeeze him through on election day.

FINANCING CAMPAIGNS

Campaign funds in such one-party states can become very important. Although thousands of legislators are chosen after spending only a few dollars, others may spend $10,000 to $20,000 or more on a campaign. During the 1964 election in California the official reports of candidates showed a total of $1,696,900 spent for campaigns for the Assembly and Senate, with as much as $42,000 reported by a single candidate for the Assembly and $64,600 by a Senate candidate. The median reported expenditure was $9,000 for Senate candidates and $6,500 for Assembly candidates. Donald Balmer's study of legislative campaign expenditures in a single Oregon county in the 1964 election revealed lower outlays, ranging from a few hundred dollars to $6,400; and in the general election campaign of 1964 ten candidates for the lower house reported a combined expenditure of $13,000. As usual, some money came from the candidates themselves, part of it from friends, and the remainder from officials of corporations and utilities and from labor unions.

A New Jersey organization has developed a systematic way of contributing to state legislators' campaigns, hoping thereby subtly to influence legislative activity. The organization is called New Jersey Organization for a Better State, abbreviated "New JOBS." Since 1959 the industrialists and businessmen in that organization have been carefully selecting candidates, regardless of party, who they think will have a chance of winning and who they believe will oppose bills that "affect costs in industry and thereby its potential for expansion." In 1965, New JOBS gave $1,000 each to 18 Senate candidates, and $750 each to 17 Assembly hopefuls, among them 22 Republicans and 13 Democrats. Carefully picking candidates who have a good chance to win, the organization backed 32 winners among its 35 beneficiaries in 1965. Its basis of selection is illustrated by its aid of a Democratic assemblyman in one county who had not joined his Democratic county colleagues in sponsoring bills on minimum wages, or unemployment and workman's compensation. Representatives of the organization claim that they do not directly approach legislators during legislative sessions to plead for any particular cause. How effective their indirect influence is no one can say, although they probably are not much less successful than those interests that give money directly and actively lobby. As far as lobbying is concerned, other agencies in agreement with New JOBS will do the persuading; it may in fact be an advantage to the giver not to appear in both roles.

In interpreting the effects of campaign contributions, an oversimplified view is often assumed, resulting in an implicit assumption that the giver has "bought" something specific. At times this does happen. For example, interest groups did purchase legislation through contributions in the most successful days of "Artie" Samish in California. Liquor, race track, and other interests provided Samish with campaign funds that he doled to legislators; and, by judicious controls over legislative leaders, Samish delivered. But this is not the customary practice in most states; nor is it in California today. Although special interests contribute to legislators who they believe share their viewpoint, or who they hope will do so, they carefully refrain from demanding a specific *quid pro quo*. After reviewing the candidates' backgrounds and records, labor unions contribute to those they hope will be pro-labor, but unions do not make a practice of directly appealing for votes because of their contributions. Most contributions go to candidates who share the contributors' point of view, and both sides consider the contribution as an effort in a common cause rather than an attempt at persuasion.

Some Rewards and Costs of Legislative Life

Perhaps the most trying aspect of a legislator's life is the frustration born of inadequate time to cope with the flood of issues and problems that a session involves. In 32 of the states the legislature meets biennially, sometimes for as long as six or nine months, but others may last less than two months. (Almost half the states in a biennium will also have special sessions, lasting from 1 to 40 legislative days.) Within that time an agenda consisting of thousands of bills must be dealt with.

In its 1963 session the Connecticut General Assembly considered over 4,000 bills, of which 1,400 were enacted. In New York, that same year the legislature passed a thousand laws from among the 9,000 bills introduced. Most legislatures are less prolific in proposing bills; the median number before legislatures in 1963 was about 2,000. But even that number can be an enormous burden, since many of them are detailed, long, and often next to impossible for a layman to comprehend. There is much specialization in the legislature, of course, and individual members perforce concentrate on a few matters of special interest to them, or that are before their committees, and then trust to colleagues' judgments on a myriad of other bills. Even to give a careful reading to all the bills that are reported out of committee may become impossible, especially late in the session when a rush of bills results from final settlement of the ultimate versions of bills.

Most legislators do not have full time to contribute to their legislative duties, it must be remembered, since their low salaries force them to hold other jobs, after a fashion, even while the legislature is in session. If the pressures of a job are not heavy for an individual member, the pressure of other legislative and political matters will consume so much of his time that he cannot give adequate consideration to a long calendar of bills. Constituents constantly call or write concerning legislation, or they ask special favors which cannot be ignored—or at least are not ignored. It may not be important to arrange for a high school class to visit the legislature, but few members will say no to a request of that kind. In addition, there are cranks who call about all manner of outlandish matters—requests to file a bill to nullify an unjust will, to investigate communist spies, etc.

Patronage matters within the jurisdiction of the legislature can consume an inordinate amount of time, as office seekers and their allies compete for low paying jobs. Even a legislator who may have little concern about party patronage may find himself deeply embroiled in such battles, either to reward a faithful campaign helper or to protect his own reputation if a dubious nominee is being proposed for his public approval. A patronage contest or a much publicized bill to outlaw dirty comic books may involve hundreds of citizen contacts for the legislator. He may have to resort, as I now confess to my erstwhile constituents that I did, to taking the telephone off the hook long enough to have dinner in peace. Then, to add another time consumer, there are innumerable social functions which a legislator is expected to grace with his presence. So he goes out four or five nights a week to testimonial dinners, lodge meetings, labor union or chamber of commerce affairs, and he addresses all groups that are anxious to have a public figure for their programs.

LACK OF STAFF ASSISTANCE

Notwithstanding the heavy load of policy-oriented work that he faces, and the short time in which to accomplish it, the average state legislator is without staff assistance to conduct research and investigations, or even to write letters. I recall that a constituent once wrote asking me to help him obtain an automobile license plate with his initials on it; he apologized for bothering me, but he wondered if my office staff could take care of it for him, when I had neither office nor staff. A corner in my hallway at home, piled high with bills, reports, and propaganda, was as near as I could come to an office; and for staff I had a part-time secretary who could barely manage to keep up with the duties assigned her by the committee of which I was chairman.

Most states have a legislative reference service of some kind, and many have legislative councils that provide research reports on issues, but there are few states that provide anything like adequate research assistance readily available to the member when he needs it. Likewise, it is rare for a state capitol to provide office space for legislators. As exceptions, California and North Carolina provide well-decorated offices for each member. California also provides secretarial assistance and $1,250 per month to maintain an office in the constituency. By not providing desperately needed help the legislature is assuredly undermining its own foundation. Legislators, as a result, are dominated by governors, bureaucracies, and lobbyists, in part because they cannot provide any alternative sources of information for substantiating their independent judgment.

LEGISLATIVE SALARIES

Whatever rewards the legislator receives for his service, they are usually not financial. Although salaries are gradually increasing (25 states have improved legislative salaries in the last decade), Table 5 indicates that, even including expense accounts, salary levels are generally low. The median salary is $1,500 a year, and for a dozen states it is $800 or less per year. At the other end of the scale a dozen states pay $4,500 a year or more (up to $12,500 in New York) and many offer additional expense allowances. If the legislator were asked to do no more than attend sessions for a few months out of the biennium, the medium range and higher salaries would seem adequate, but special sessions and other necessary political and legislative duties during the non-session months also place demands on the time of legislators. Only wealthy or retired legislators can afford to make the legislature their full-time career.

SHADY INCOME

It must be admitted, however, that some legislators do not restrict themselves to their salaries when counting their income from legislative service. Although the open purchase of votes by lobbyists, as practiced in the late nineteenth century, is no longer common, the rough equivalent of the practice is not dead by any means. Periodically the press reports crooked manipulations by legislators and from time to time one goes to jail for it, although more rarely than probably deserved. "Legal" payoffs through public relations fees, or legal counsel fees are often reported to be involved in moving legislation forward in some states.

Paul Simon, the Illinois legislator who claimed that one-third of his colleagues accepted payoffs, said that lobbyists had been advised that it would cost them from $200 to $500 to bring bills out of committee. Race tracks in Illinois and many other states have made notorious deals with legislators in order to protect their interests. One legislative leader in Illinois was reported to have been allowed to purchase race-track shares at ten cents per share, which produced a return of $23,000; when queried by a reporter about the deal, the leader was quoted as saying, "The only mistake I made was that I didn't get more." The influence of the tracks is also demonstrated by the action of the Illinois legislature to *cut* race-track taxes on the same day that the sales tax was increased. Illinois is not the only state that has given cause for concern about the moral level of legislatures—Louisiana, Massachusetts, Rhode Island, Texas, and other states have provided their share. This kind of behavior does not by any means appear to be universal, but it requires only a few rotten apples to give the barrel its aroma.

There are potential rewards for service in the legislature, other than

Table 5: 1963 Legislative Salaries and Expense Allowances.*

State	Daily Pay		Biennial Salary	Daily or Biennial Expense Allowances
	Amount	No. of Days Permitted		
Alabama	$10	36		$20
Alaska			$ 5,000	35
Arizona			3,600	12
Arkansas	20	60		
California			12,000	20 + $2,400 per biennium
Colorado			6,400	
Connecticut			2,000	500 per biennium
Delaware			6,000	
Florida			2,400	25
Georgia	10			40
Hawaii			4,000	32.50-45.00
Idaho	10	60		
Illinois			12,000	
Indiana			3,600	
Iowa	30			
Kansas	10	120		15
Kentucky				25
Louisiana	50	90		250 per month when not in session
Maine			1,600	
Maryland			3,600†	2,400 per biennium
Massachusetts			15,600	1,200 per biennium
Michigan			14,000†	2,500 per biennium
Minnesota			4,800	12-18
Mississippi			3,000	100 per month when not in session
Missouri			9,600	10
Montana	20	60		
Nebraska			4,800	
Nevada	25	60		15
New Hampshire			200	
New Jersey			10,000	1,000 per biennium for secretarial aid
New Mexico	20	60		
New York			20,000†	2,000 per biennium
North Carolina	15	60		12

Table 5 (continued)

State	Daily Pay		Biennial Salary	Daily or Biennial Expense Allowances
	Amount	No. of Days Permitted		
North Dakota	5	60		20
Ohio			10,000	
Oklahoma	15	75		
Oregon			6,000	
Pennsylvania			12,000	6,000 per biennium
Rhode Island	5	60		
South Carolina			3,600	15
South Dakota			3,000	
Tennessee	10	75		5
Texas			9,600	12
Utah			1,000	5
Vermont (85 per week)				
Virginia			1,080	720 per biennium
Washington			2,400	25
West Virginia			3,000	
Wisconsin			10,800	25-40 per month when not in session; additional for larger districts
Wyoming	12	40		20

* Omits stationery, postage, and similar allowances.
† Since 1963 the salaries of these states have been increased:
  Maryland to $4,800, Michigan to $20,000, New York to $25,000.
Source: Council of State Governments, Book of the States, *1964-65.*

the present monetary returns. The ambitious lawyer may find that the free publicity in his home town is an enormous asset to his law practice. Some are given lucrative positions following their legislative careers. Others return to lobby among their one-time colleagues. A few accept positions in industry and business that look suspiciously like rewards for loyalty while in the legislature. Some win political jobs outside the legislature as a reward for their party loyalty and service.

NONMONETARY REWARDS

There are also other satisfactions in legislative service. The deference —both genuine and spurious—paid to legislators is heady stuff, and many legislators find it exhilarating to be in the spotlight as they never have been before. In a broader perspective it may be a little matter, but to a small-town legislator it can be highly rewarding to be featured from time to time in the local newspaper. Such evidences of esteem may become a major reason why legislators return to the legislature despite the trying aspects of the job. Naturally this kind of motivation has risks; it produces some pompous nonentities who serve for small-time glory more than any other reason. But even for the most dedicated and able legislator the psychic rewards are important.

To win a seat in the legislature is also to gain an opportunity to influence policy in some desired way, and that too is an attraction. Some legislators have a burning sense of cause about waste in government and devote themselves wholeheartedly to budget paring. Some arrive bent on serving the working man, the poor, minorities, and the disadvantaged. They may find that it is impossible to generate enough power to do much about improving the conditions of patients in mental hospitals or changing educational policies, but at least the opportunity to fight from the inside for desired objectives is afforded.

Less noble motives can also move individuals to desire a legislative seat. A good many members arrive determined to promote the welfare of the industry or profession in which they are involved. The man who owns a trucking company may have a single-minded interest in cutting taxes on trucking. The employee of an insurance company may come to do battle for lowering taxes on insurance and protecting the insurance business. A liquor dealer, race-track employee, or a labor leader may have little else in mind than promotion of the interest he represents. The direct reward to the individual may or may not be significant, but it is obvious that the opportunity to serve some relatively limited objective of this kind does motivate many legislators.

Interest-group Conflict and Conflicts of Interest

It usually surprises a new legislator, whatever the degree of his commitment to particular or general interests, that the legislature is an arena of swirling conflicts among interest groups, and conflicts of enormous scope and often high intensity. All kinds of organized interest groups—and they are legion—and many *ad hoc* groups formed to fight temporary battles come to the legislature to win special advantages or to protect vested interests. They range from historical societies and conservation groups on the one side to business groups and gambling syndicates on the other. The law can become a significant factor in the success of a particular segment of the economy, and therefore every effort is made to assure appropriate legislative action. This is obvious in contests over the levying of taxes. Industry wants the burden to be on the individual taxpayer; retailers want to avoid the sales tax; particular industries want to cut or eliminate specific taxes on their products; alternatively, they seek the "earmarking" of taxes so that the income from a particular tax will go only to serve the interest of the paying group. In this respect, the combined efforts of the highway lobby have won legislative agreement in most states to limit the expenditure of the returns on gasoline taxes to highway purposes. Sportsmen try to have all funds from hunting and fishing licenses earmarked so that the funds can only be used to regulate and improve hunting and fishing.

USING LAW FOR COMPETITIVE ADVANTAGE

Innumerable attempts are made to improve the competitive position of one economic interest at the expense of another. Drug stores seek the privilege of selling liquor and the liquor dealers object. Liquor dealers fight for state minimum prices to protect themselves against the price-cutting competition of such larger retailers as department stores. Large garages attempt to prevent filling stations from doing automotive repairs. Insurance companies attempt to ban the sale of automobile insurance by auto dealers. The whole gamut of licensing legislation offers opportunities to freeze out competitors by restricting entry into an occupation through setting absurdly high standards for entry. All this is done, ostensibly, in the interest of the public—to assure protection from inferior service, to protect the health and safety of society. But underneath, even to a naïve observer, lies the naked cupidity of one element in competition with others.

The pressures that can develop around some of these contests are enormous and extremely taxing to the legislator who may have no burning interests in hairdressing schools or in the qualifications of various kinds of engineers. Whether interested or not, he will be badgered by lobbyists, subjected to pleading by interested constituents, and harangued by his much-involved colleagues to whom the contest has personal significance. No small part of this pressure derives from the officials, and especially the professional staff members, of the organized interests. It is to their advantage to make a wide segment of the interest-group constituency aware of the issue, for by doing so they call attention to the importance of the organization. If the battle is won, they can point to the importance of the organization to the economic well being of the members. If it is lost, they can plan a new campaign to win in the future. Either way, the importance of the organization is stressed, and thereby the future salaries of the lobbyists are guaranteed.

An illustration of such attempts to involve the membership of an organization was the hassle over a bill in Connecticut to prevent auto dealers from selling insurance to their purchasers. During the day on which the Senate was to vote on the issue and, indeed, during a long debate between several insurancemen-senators and a car dealer-senator, the lobbyist for the state's car dealers paced the floor behind the brass rail separating the senators from spectators and lobbyists. He was clearly worried. After a brief disappearance he returned and resumed his pacing. Messengers shortly began delivering telegrams to each senator from car dealers in their districts. All pleaded for the defeat of the bill. When the vote was taken, the bill was defeated; whether the telegrams had much to do with the outcome no one can state with accuracy. A few days later I happened to see one of the dealers whose name was signed to one of my telegrams, and I told him I had voted as he wished. (I didn't tell him it was *because* he wished it, for it was not.) The car dealer looked at me in surprise, and asked, "What telegram?"

A classic illustration of the pressure on legislators which involved fraud was the long fight between the railroads and truckers in Pennsylvania, where the railroads attempted to curtail the weight loads that trucks were permitted to carry. Front organizations were created to plead the railroads' case, fraudulent "scientific" reports on the damage done to roads by trucks were presented, and, among other gimmicks, the railroads even persuaded soap opera writers to present truck drivers as mean and despicable characters in their "dramas." All this came to light when a disgruntled secretary quit the public relations firm handling the promotion and took with her enough evidence to justify a suit on grounds of unfair competition under the Sherman Anti-Trust Law. The suit was won in lower court, but was subsequently reversed.

It is also a surprise to the new and inexperienced legislator that such battles are often fought with intense bitterness and at times with highly unethical tactics. On the surface, legislative contesting is conducted under Marquis of Queensbury style rules, seemingly orderly and polite. Behind the scenes the prevailing rules are sometimes those of an alley brawl. At times any advantage will be taken. The innocent member may find that a wholly unrelated piece of legislation in which he is interested is hopelessly stalled, and there is assurance that it will stay stalled until enough votes are corralled to move along another particular bill. Local bills wanted by communities in a member's district are often held hostage by the legislator-tools of lobbyists in order to apply needed pressure.

An illustration of this is provided by the *Philadelphia Bulletin* of September 19, 1965. A Pennsylvania legislator backing a particular highway development program held for bargaining purposes a bill that would restore a seventeenth century historical site. Some leaders of the historical group were opposed to the representative's much desired highway, so he persuaded the committee chairman having jurisdiction over the restoration bill to have it recalled to committee from the floor—despite the fact that the committee chairman was a Democrat and the interceder a Republican. The representative said he wasn't opposed to the restoration bill and hoped it would pass, but that he wanted to teach them a "little lesson in politics." Accordingly, he asked them to send to the highway commissioner a letter stating approval of the highway project. One leader of the restoration group reported that the representative had demanded copies of these letters, and if they were satisfactory, "you get your $21,000" for the project; if not, no money.

Often the legislature will, in effect, withdraw from conflicts among interest groups and encourage the contestants to reach an amicable resolution of differences and then return to the legislature for ratification of the agreement. This is most likely to happen when the conflict directly involves no public agency and when there are few if any legislators who are deeply committed on the issue. Such abdication may be reprehensible, but when there are more conflicts than can be handled, a suggestion that one of them be resolved by someone else is often welcome.

INSIDE LOBBYING

As mentioned in an earlier discussion of "rewards" to the legislator for his service, there is a widespread practice of "inside lobbying" by interested legislators. Few of those involved sense any conflict of interest whatsoever. On the contrary, the inside lobbyist-legislator says he is merely bringing his own expertise to bear on the matter. Does the insurance man not know intimately the problems of his business? Why should he not involve himself in a bill that affects his interests when he can "explain" the matter to those in education, law, or retail business? He points out that after all he is ready to allow the same privilege to others, and does not complain when the banker, labor leader, or lawyer pleads his case. It is true that he does have special knowledge and that in some cases on technically complicated matters this knowledge is indispensable to the less informed members. Nevertheless, it is difficult to draw a line between technical assistance and self-interest promotion.

Some inside lobbyists refuse to acknowledge that they are in any sense promoting a special interest. Schoolteachers in the legislature will often vehemently deny that their arduous work for better schools, and perhaps even for higher teachers' salaries, is the same thing as the real estate man's fight for strict licensing laws on the privilege of selling real estate. The interest may be far from pernicious, and it may not be especially selfish, but the practice does involve the use of an inside position to further a group interest.

LAWYER-LEGISLATORS

There is some debate about the extent to which lawyers are guilty of using their privileged position in the legislature to further the interests of the legal profession. Much complaint is heard about their tendency to do so, especially from non-lawyer legislators who sometimes resent the advantage in familiarity with the language and usages of the law that the attorney brings with him. There is a kind of helpless dependence on the lawyer's skills which other legislators at once appreciate and resent. Accordingly, there are claims that the lawyer-legislators try to write the law to increase the dependence upon legal skills in carrying it out. The late Governor Herbert Lehman has been quoted by Heinz Eulau and John D. Sprague in *Lawyers in Politics* as complaining of "the conspiracy of lawyer-legislators to perpetrate for their profession the obstructions to justice by which it prospers." Legislators have claimed that lawyers "try to win lawsuits in the legislature that they can't win in court" and that they "draw up laws so nobody including themselves can understand them. It makes business for them."

Some scholars have attempted to disprove this charge by showing that lawyers do not form an identifiable voting bloc in the legislature. In particular, David Derge demonstrated the absence of such a cluster-bloc of lawyer votes. By studying the lawyer in the Indiana General Assembly he found, for example, that lawyers' votes on fifteen bills concerning fees in civil practice and the organization of the state court system divided about the same as non-lawyer votes on all but one of the bills. On the latter bill—one to allow attorneys to collect separate fees for services in estate matters—the lawyers divided roughly two to one in favor; but the bill failed of passage. It would have passed had four lawyers changed their votes. "One must conclude," Derge says, "that there is no 'lawyer bloc' in roll calls involving public policy intimately related to the practice of law."

The fact that evidence of roll-call blocs is difficult to find does not mean that there is no self-serving activity by lawyers. Lawyers dominate —often to the exclusion of all non-lawyers—judiciary committees, to which are referred a wide variety of bills (and, in some states, nominations) that involve interests close to lawyers' professional concerns. Having served on the Connecticut judiciary committee (the only non-lawyer senator on the committee), I am well aware that decisions were often made in terms of the interest of the legal profession. This does not mean that there was a pernicious conspiracy to take advantage of the rest of society by promoting legal fees before all else; but lawyers are human and they err on the side of "safety" in making sure that bills do not impair their professional interests. A discussion of the issue of whether the public defender system should be expanded is not conducted as purely a matter of the adequacy of the legal service provided for the indigent; comments also are made about the needs of the young lawyer as well as the older ones who are not doing well and who can benefit from the fees that assigned counsel collect when the public defender is not used. I have also heard vigorous argument among lawyer-legislators about fee provisions in statutes that were anything but selfless pleas for justice.

I have never seen evidence that lawyers consciously attempt to complicate statutes in order to generate legal disputes; indeed, the evidence I have seen would appear to suggest the opposite. A legally trained mind is often a traditionally oriented mind that places great value in time-tested phraseology and approaches, and it is possible that without conscious effort to complicate laws the complication comes "naturally." Thus, the legal profession, like others, tends to use its inside position to some extent to serve its own interests, whatever may be the slimness of the roll-call evidence to support the charge.

Is there a "solution" to the problem of the insider lobbyist? Probably not, as long as the legislator is necessarily a part-time functionary who has only a minimum chance to separate his interest concerns from his legislative concerns. Since he is actively engaged in his profession at the time he is legislating and is constantly associating with others who are actively engaged in coping with the problems of the interest, it is difficult to see how the distinction can readily be made.

The practice is common in the United States Congress where the members are full-time legislators, often with little thought about ever being for the remainder of a career anything but a politician. Yet the self-serving efforts to promote interests with which the congressman or senator is involved are widely reported. At least they are deplored by some members of Congress and by some part of the public as well. It is rare for a state legislator to make this kind of complaint and urge a code of ethics to suppress conflict of interest, although such a proposal has often been made in Congress—admittedly without result thus far. Given the lack of consciousness of the problem at the state level, either by the public or legislators, there is no reason to expect the early establishment of a code that might tend to suppress the more flagrant kinds of conflict of interest.

Concluding Thoughts on the Role of the Individual Legislator

Although there are wide variations among the states in the role of individual legislators—and in the kind of legislators elected—there are valid generalizations that can be made about the over-all problems that the individual faces. First, he is often an amateur, struggling, sometimes not very successfully, to cope with an alien and bewildering world. His ignorance may make him an unwitting pawn of others—legislative leaders, lobbyists, chief executives, or bureaucrats.

Second, he is overworked and underpaid. Short sessions and long agendas, intense pressures, and many highly complicated questions to be resolved make legislative life hectic and often frustrating. Since the legislature is understaffed, the member has no one on whom to rely for technical assistance and much needed research with which to assert legislative independence. He has the services of a bill drafting staff in nearly all states, but he often needs much more than the translation of his ideas into statute form. He needs to know what other jurisdictions have done when faced with the problem with which he is wrestling, what have been the consequences of a particular law in other states, what rationale can be found for a proposal that he wants to make, or what may be the costs and implications of a proposal urged by the state bureaucracy or an interest group. Unless he knows these answers before he comes to the legislature he is not likely to have the time or perhaps the ability to ascertain them for himself while facing the multiplicity of legislative duties.

He is also, significantly, a politician—one who has some skills in interpersonal negotiations, and an ability to compromise in order to resolve an issue. This is not always reckoned as an asset for the legislator, but without this quality it is difficult to see how he could be at all effective in the legislative arena as it exists today. Outsiders often ask legislators how they can bear to vote for a compromise version of a bill that they have fought for in its pristine form. How could half a loaf be so acceptable? The answer is obvious. It is the legislator's function to deal in half-loaves. If he cannot get the million dollars he wants for a retarded children's hospital program, he will usually settle reluctantly for half a million, knowing that refusal may either doom the half-million-dollar program or may mark him among his colleagues as a man who cannot see more than one set of objectives—his own. To anyone who holds dear the preservation of forests or the protection of the helpless in state institutions, it is sometimes difficult to comprehend the single-minded concern of others with highway building or economic development. But the legislature is where all these diverse sets of interests collide and a legislator who cannot have some empathy for others with different values is as useful as a saloon-keeper would be at a WCTU convention. The successful legislator is a politician in the best sense of the word—one who can see and moderate different points of view and learn to compromise when it is necessary and to refuse to when it is not.

To what extent can changes in legislative procedure, length of terms, salaries, staff assistance, and other matters correct the difficulties of the individual legislator to which we have referred? To what extent, in fact, is it possible to halt the slow decline in effectiveness and in prestige of the state legislature by making such changes? The experience of many states with reforms like these should stand as clear warning that the alteration of surface aspects of legislative life will not remedy many of the deep problems that stem from the political ethos of the states. If irresponsibility and self-serving practices suffuse a state legislature, as they do in some states, all the structural reforms imaginable will cure nothing. For example, longer sessions will not correct the problem any better than the shorter sessions did, which our predecessors proposed as a way of curtailing legislative mischief.

I return to the point made earlier, quoting from James D. Barber about the "lawmaker" legislator. If political organizations, in their recruiting of candidates, were to seek lawmaker types, and if the political ethos allowed the resulting legislators to make the most of their opportunities for service, structural and procedural reforms would help prevent the further decline of the legislature. Without capable legislators, and lacking a state political ethos that would sustain them, the state legislature will wither away, or perhaps will come to resemble another House of Lords, full of pomp and empty of meaning.

John C. Wahlke

5

Organization and Procedure

Debate over governmental organization and procedure is more popular in America than in most countries. Our understanding of state legislative organization and procedure will profit, however, if we bear in mind an important characteristic shared by all American state legislatures: each is a separate and distinct institutionalized group, with its own established way of doing business.

State Legislatures as Political Institutions

What do we mean when we call a state legislature a "political institution"? Most importantly, the term implies that members of a legislature are not just a random assembly of individuals, each guided only by his own notions or the wishes of constituents and others outside the legislature. Rather, they are men whose common membership in the legislature obliges them to act in certain ways and within certain limits. They know that the legislature has its own ways of doing things and that whatever they wish to do, they must do it more or less in the ways the legislative group recognizes as legitimate.

To recognize that the legislature is a political institution is to recognize that legislators do not enjoy the luxury of political free will. Legislators are often unjustly criticized by people who want them to do one thing or another but who fail to see that what they ask would run legislators headlong against some powerful institutional constraint. Particularly if

JOHN C. WAHLKE *is Professor of Political Science at the University of Iowa. His many publications include* The Legislative System: Explorations in Legislative Behavior (*with Heinz Eulau, William Buchanan, and LeRoy C. Ferguson*), Loyalty in a Democratic State, *and* Legislative Behavior: A Reader in Theory and Research (*with Heinz Eulau*).

we are thinking of changing the organization and procedure by which the legislature does its business we should be aware of the character of these institutional constraints.

LEGISLATIVE OFFICE AND ROLE

To say that legislators occupy the *office* of legislator is to say they are expected to perform the *role* of legislator. We—as citizens, spectators, and constituents—expect them to act in certain ways and not in others. In turn, legislators have similar expectations of themselves and of each other. It is in such expectations, in legislators' notions of the kinds of behavior that are legitimately associated with their office and role of legislator, and of the kinds that are not, that we can actually "see" the organization and procedure of a legislature. If there were no patterns of behavior firmly established by the notion of legislative office and role there would in truth be no legislature, but only a temporary assembly of individuals, each ignorant and uncertain about why he was there and what he or others might do next.

These patterns or rules of expected behavior, even for legislators, are peculiarly abstract and beyond reach at any given moment. Members readily sense that individual legislators come and go, but "the legislature" remains substantially unchanged over long periods of time. They sense a succession of individuals with different backgrounds, conceptions, and wishes, each rapidly conforming to the expected patterns of behavior, which are therefore preserved from legislative generation to generation. It is correct to say that "the institution" thus imposes its rules of behavior on the members. However, few legislators really feel imposed upon in the process, because most recognize the great advantage of beginning each session with already established patterns that old members can readily follow and new members can easily learn.

The legislative role is not a mere set of verbal instructions to be memorized. The rules are not only embodied in legislators' conscious thoughts; they are built into their unthinking habits and into the customs of the legislative body. Legislators do not have to read the constitution or the rules of procedure and then consciously remind themselves that they should, for example, submit bills in a certain form, at a certain time, or address themselves to "Mr. Speaker" when they want to speak on the floor. These, and innumerable other rules, are known and followed almost without thinking. They appear to members to be part of a complex legislative culture in which it is their business to be at home because they are legislators.

Like all cultures, legislative cultures are highly specific to the particular group. That is, members of an American state legislature are rarely much concerned with similarities and differences between their own way of doing things and those of other state legislatures. They learn uniquely the ways of their own legislative group and they think of those ways as uniquely a property of that group. An American state legislator does not learn generally how to be *a* legislator; he learns how to be *the* gentleman from X county in the representative body of *the* State of Y. If some supposedly "better" way of doing something is suggested to the members of any American state legislature, they will all likely ask first whether or not it is consistent with "the way we do things in *this* chamber," that is, how it affects the legislative culture they accept as the premise for all their legislative actions.

FORMAL AND INFORMAL RULES OF ACTION AND CONDUCT

The rules of behavior that form the legislative culture and guide behavior originate in various ways and at different times. Some of them are formal, expressly set forth in rules of procedure, constitutions, and other authoritative documents. For example, state constitutions tell legislators, in effect, when they must come to the capitol and when they may leave, by specifying the times for holding legislative sessions. Formally adopted rules of procedures tell legislators when they may propose changes in wording of bills, when they may seek to defeat bills by substituting others for them, when and how they may introduce amendments, and so on. Constitutions and rules of procedure also describe the outlines of legislative organization when, for example, they prescribe the creating and main functions of such legislative officers as Speaker or Committee Chairman.

But in no case do such formal rules even begin to describe fully the way legislatures operate. Such formal rules and prescriptions are always amplified by unwritten (therefore "informal") understandings which have equally decisive effect on legislators' behavior. Sometimes formal rules are in fact superseded by informal rules. The best known of many possible examples (notably the U. S. Congress) is the informal rule of seniority, by which some legislatures invariably make the majority-party member with longest service on a committee chairman of that committee, even while appearing to elect chairmen by majority vote, as the formal rule requires.

In recent years we have recognized more clearly that the informal rules of behavior are at least as numerous, as clearly recognized, and as controlling in legislators' minds as the formal rules. A 1957 study of several state legislatures (published as *The Legislative System*) identified at least forty-two specific informal rules of action and conduct followed by legislators in those states. Included were such rules as abstaining from any discussion of local bills affecting only their sponsor's district, abstaining from criticism or ridicule of a member before his visiting constituents in the chamber, and speaking on subjects only when technically or politically informed on them. Significantly, these informal rules were supported by informal sanctions, such as blocking legislation introduced by consistent violators of informal, or formal, rules.

Legislative organization and procedure, then, is essentially a body of established patterns of behavior that delimit offices within a legislature, ways of filling those offices, and acceptable modes of conduct both for legislative officers and for rank-and-file members. To understand legislative organization or procedure fully means to recognize the controlling patterns of behavior, the limits of acceptable conduct, and both the formal and informal rules which make those patterns. It is not enough merely to locate a sentence or paragraph in a written body of rules; that may even be quite misleading. By the same token, to change legislative organization or procedure means more than just rewriting a sentence or a paragraph; it means altering established patterns of behavior.

In the next four sections of this chapter we shall examine some of the patterns of organization and procedure commonly found among the states, keeping in mind that it is patterns of behavior in which we are interested and not merely verbal prescriptions. In the final section of the chapter we shall consider some of the proposals for changing these patterns and the proposed ways of bringing about such changes.

The Mobilization of Legislative Manpower

Like any other human enterprise, an American state legislature is what the character and quality of its personnel permit it to be. In this section we are concerned with ways in which various organizational and procedural patterns and rules may affect the character of the legislative body, by determining to some degree the kinds of people who become members.

QUALIFICATIONS FOR LEGISLATIVE OFFICE

It may safely be said that formal prerequisites for the office of state legislator no longer influence significantly the character of legislative membership. It is not quite correct to say that anyone who may vote may also become a state legislator if he can win an election, but it is not far wrong. Even as did colonial assemblies before America won independence, American state legislatures early displayed a steady elimination of one restriction on eligibility to membership after another. Two requirements—that a legislator own a certain amount of property or pay a certain amount of taxes, and that he belong to a certain church or not belong to certain others—lasted in a few states as much as twenty or thirty years after Independence. But, by and large, the major formal barriers to membership in state legislatures had fallen shortly after states drew up their constitutions.

There are still membership restrictions in some state legislatures that are probably not known by most voters in those states. Ministers of the gospel, for example, are excluded in a number of states; known duellists are excluded in at least one. In both cases the exclusion is by formal constitutional provision. It is not the formality of exclusion, however, which accounts for the fact that few, if any, such persons are found in modern state legislatures. These are "exclusions" that no longer really exclude anyone.

As in the case of voting, and for substantially the same political reasons, membership in the legislature is now subject to only one principal qualification, that of age. But age requirements for eligibility to membership in a lower house are in all but a few states the same as the age requirement for voting. For upper houses, in a number of states, they are slightly higher. There have been cases in recent years in which a duly elected individual has been prevented from assuming his seat because of failure to meet the age requirement, but on the whole it can hardly be said that the character of legislative membership collectively, in any state, appears to be significantly altered by age requirements.

Far more important than formal requirements in setting the character of legislative membership are the informal determinants mentioned previously (Chapter 4). Women, for example, are not excluded, but they are hardly present in numbers proportional to the general population. Even more "unrepresented," although equally eligible in formal terms (even in southern states), are Negroes and other ethnic minorities. As we have seen, certain occupational groups (such as lawyers) and certain social groups (middle to upper income, for example) are also "over-represented" in American state legislatures. But in none of these instances is it formal qualifications for office or formal procedures for choosing legislators which determine the composition of the legislative bodies. Far more influential is the play of social, psychological, economic, and political factors. It follows that to recruit different kinds of people into our legislatures would require more than formal changes in constitutions or statutes.

TERMS AND TENURE

As in the case of the United States Congress, the term of office for senators in most state legislatures is longer than the term of representatives in the lower house. Two years is the prevailing term in the lower houses, with only Alabama, Louisiana, Maryland, and Mississippi having four-year terms. But in thirty-six states senators serve four-year terms. In many of these states the terms are overlapping, as are the terms of United States senators.

Insofar as there have been changes in the term of office in recent years these have all been in the direction of making terms of representatives longer. Michigan (for its senate) and Nebraska (for its single house) several years ago increased terms from two to four years, and Georgia has considered a similar lengthening of terms. The principal argument for making terms longer has been the hope that such a change would lessen the high turnover in legislative membership at each election, thereby promoting stability and experienced performance and diminishing the time spent in "breaking in" new members every session. It is obvious that increasing a two-year term to four years would automatically double the tenure in the case of those numerous legislators who serve one term only and then choose not to run for another.

There is little evidence, however, as to whether or not changing the length of term would affect the average duration of service in any other way. Indeed, the kind of person who now finds one term more than enough might be discouraged from serving at all by the thought of a four-year term. On the other hand, it is certainly conceivable that persons compelled by their term of office to serve four years might in that time become sufficiently acclimated or attuned to legislative life to seek continuation of it. Certainly tenure of senators is, on the average, greater than tenure of the shorter-term representatives.

In either case, we have much less genuine information than we need about the actual consequences of either longer or shorter tenure on the performance of legislators. On the face of it we should expect more effective service from the experienced "old hand," thoroughly acquainted through long service as a legislator with the people and processes of state government, than from the "green-horn," arriving in the capitol for the first time with only a meager notion of what the legislature does or how it does it. As Duane Lockard has noted, however, experience might well lead in some cases to "more refined means of bargaining and dealing for personally desired ends." At least both views seem to agree that longer terms should produce greater experience in some respect.

STAFF AND ASSISTANCE

We saw in the previous chapter that legislative salaries are not such that pay and perquisites alone will attract men to legislative office. Legislators probably feel more strongly about being provided inadequate staff and assistance than about low salaries and inadequate allowances for direct, out-of-pocket expenses of their daily work. For most legislators no experience is more frustrating than the enormous gap between what constituents and public seem to expect and what they see as possible to do with the facilities available.

The average United States congressman feels harried even though he has an office at the capitol staffed by a fair number of administrative assistants, secretaries, stenographers, legislative interns, and other helpers. In only a very few states do state legislators have even a secretary. A common arrangement for clerical service during sessions is for several administrative agencies to provide "on loan" a stenographer or two, who collectively form a stenographic pool to which legislators can turn. Needless to say, this arrangement hardly encourages the legislators to engage in numerous, frequent, or lengthy correspondence with persons in or outside of their constituencies. Equally needless to say, constituents rarely recognize this limitation or, when they do, accept it as a legitimate excuse for missing or infrequent replies to their queries.

To have an executive assistant to perform minor research (such as getting information relevant to proposed legislation, or information for constituents), a state legislator would need to find the capable person to employ, find the place for him to work, and pay him wholly from his own funds. Even if he could do all that, he would probably find his aide getting short shrift from many official agencies which tend to think of the state legislator as either not needing or not deserving such assistance.

In all states there are agencies to which the legislator can go for some services as he needs them. But these are not at all "his" in the way staff and secretarial assistance would be. And he must learn, if he is a new legislator, which of the many services he needs are actually available, and where, and which are not. For example, in almost every state the individual legislator can secure legal advice in drafting bills. But in some states this service is available primarily through the attorney general's office, in others through a legislative reference service, in still others through a legislative counsel, and so on. In all cases he must learn the political consequences of using one alternative source of legal counsel as against another. Some "counsel" may be highly colored by the political preferences of the agency giving the advice, while other counsel may be quite narrowly technical in nature. Many states maintain state libraries and most states have legislative reference libraries which individual legislators may use, but even the very best of these do not provide facilities or services comparable to those provided congressmen through the Library of Congress.

To a surprising degree, therefore, every American state legislature depends upon individual legislators taking on a variety of tedious and frequently menial chores. Notes must be written in longhand and delivered in person by legislators. Telephone calls consume more time since they must be placed by legislators and not by secretaries. Each legislature is in a sense a body of lone, unaided individuals who organize themselves as best they can to do the business of the legislature.

SIZE

Even before sociologists and social psychologists documented the fact, it was known that the way people operate together depends somewhat on the number involved. With respect to legislatures, it is fairly obvious that a body of several hundred persons can discuss any matter only if almost every member agrees to say almost nothing. It is less obvious, but equally important, that personal and informal methods of dealing with its business are more possible for small than for large groups. Genuine deliberation is possible among a few people; a mass meeting can only listen to harangues.

American state legislatures range in size almost from mass meetings to small groups. Senates are invariably the smaller of a state's two houses, ranging in size from Nevada's seventeen to sixty-seven in Minnesota, as compared with lower chambers ranging from thirty-five in Delaware to New Hampshire's four hundred. Nebraska's unicameral legislature has forty-nine members.

While there have been a number of changes in the number of seats in state legislatures, particularly as a result of reapportionment in recent years, there have been few dramatic changes of scale. Thus, changes in senates made during the 1962-63 biennium produced an addition of 60 seats in twelve states and a decrease of seven seats in two. It was estimated that lower houses changed by an addition of 101 seats in eight states and a decrease of 77 in seven. The largest increase, proportionately speaking, was that in Idaho's House, which over several terms moved from 59 to 79.

These changes of size, while proportionately small in magnitude, reveal something about the process of changing legislative organization. The fact that they are small indicates that long-established patterns, grounded in the earliest years of state constitution-making, are the principal controlling factors, and that the changes made are only minor adjustments in those long-established patterns. The small legislatures of generations ago are the small legislatures of today; the king-sized legislatures of the last century are still the largest. We have suggested that size itself is a factor with observable consequences for legislative performance. But in no case of the changes actually made or proposed were such considerations taken into account in proposing or opposing the changes in size. In most instances, changes in size were made whenever such changes made it easy to accommodate the various considerations urged in the course of reapportionment controversies.

Legislative "Plant" and Facilities

Just as an industry's potential to produce is limited ultimately by its available plant capacity, so a legislature's potential for doing its job is governed in some fashion by the available legislative "plant." Legislative manpower may be hamstrung in hopelessly inadequate physical facilities, just as skilled industrial workmen may be cramped in obsolete plants with improper equipment. Conversely, just as industrial ingenuity on the part of management and skilled craftsmen can maximize the possibilities for useful service in backward facilities, so too can imaginative effort by both leadership and rank-and-file legislators get the most out of backward legislative facilities.

LEGISLATIVE CHAMBERS

Both legislators and the general public tend to consider the question of legislative work space a matter long since settled by historical and architectural accident. Each legislative body meets in a chamber historically set aside for that purpose. Few wonder what notions of legislative purpose guided construction of the chamber in its inception or whether those notions are relevant to today's needs.

Traditionally, state legislators have been provided with a desk and chair on the floor, but little else. Inasmuch as the size of legislative bodies has changed very little, minor rearrangements of seats have readily accommodated such changes in membership as have occurred. It is interesting that styles in legislative furniture on the floor have likewise changed but little. Legislators' desks in most instances have but one small drawer, adequate to hold a few pencils and a few memo pads. Exact data are not available, but from casual observation it would seem that many legislatures still provide a cuspidor at each desk, or, in more modernized chambers, disposable plastic liners for waste baskets.

The traditional Speaker's podium, flanked or fronted by desks or tables for clerks and other workers, is set off with varying degrees of physical separation from the body of legislative desks in all chambers. The legislative body is separated from the public audience by guard rails and gates at the back and sides in most but not all chambers. Most chambers have a gallery for the public still more clearly separated from the legislators. But state legislatures tend to be less rigid about excluding nonlegislators from the floor than do national bodies like the United States Congress or the British Parliament. In some states interested constituents and other laymen come and go almost as freely as legislators, and sit regularly with them at their desks.

The seating arrangement in most cases is semicircular, facing the Speaker's dais, or rectangular, approximating this arrangement. In most chambers, as in the United States Congress, the two parties sit on different sides of the semicircle. Such an arrangement, of course, is not found in nonpartisan states. Questions of physical arrangement and seating plans are not simply aesthetic matters, without political consequence, even though consideration of political effects has rarely entered into the design of legislative chambers. Sir Winston Churchill argued vehemently, when plans for rebuilding the war-damaged House of Commons were under discussion after World War II, that the historic British arrangement, whereby Government and Opposition Members face each other from opposite sides of a rectangular chamber, is far more effective than the continental and the common American semicircular arrangement in promoting confrontation of opposing views, clarification of issues, and intelligent political debate. It has similarly been argued that the theater-like array of row on row of seats facing a stage, as used in the U.S.S.R. and elsewhere, tends to turn legislative debates into a series of speeches at a passive legislative audience. In any event, it is likely that the character of legislative discussion and debate is in some unmeasurable degree influenced by the physical layout of the legislative chamber.

The only significant changes in legislative physical facilities since colonial times have been the adoption in many states of time- and labor-saving devices which help legislators to do somewhat more efficiently, but in substantially the same way as before, the things they have traditionally done. Most chambers of any size are now equipped with loudspeakers and with microphones at or near each desk. This not only makes it easier for modern legislators to follow proceedings, and for the average legislator to make some impact even if he is not endowed with a silver tongue and leather lungs, but it probably also makes floor proceedings more important by making it harder for legislators to ignore them while doing other business at their desks. The fact that legislators' microphones are usually controlled from the Speaker's desk also makes it much easier for the presiding officer to manage debate and recognize whom he wishes.

The most notable adaptation of electronic gadgetry by modern legislatures, of course, is the electric roll-call voting machine now in use in most lower houses and many senates. The saving of time by a machine which instantly records and tabulates votes when legislators activate switches at their desks, as compared with the name-by-name call of the roll by a clerk, with pauses for late-voters, repetitions of misunderstood votes, and the other minor inconveniences of *viva-voce* voting, is obvious. Instant roll calls also make it more difficult, but still not altogether impossible, for a legislator to vote in specific reaction to the votes of colleagues or leaders whose vote is proclaimed before his own name is called. The printed tabulation produced by electric roll-call voting machines also provides a new type of legislative record, making it easier to remember accurately what happened in any given roll call and more difficult to make changes after the fact. In this connection, we might also note that one or two chambers now supplement the written legislative record with complete tape recordings of the floor proceedings of the entire legislative session. But there is little evidence that such an electronic record is of significant help or hindrance to legislators, however much historical researchers might favor them.

OTHER PHYSICAL FACILITIES

In all but a few cases, the legislative chambers are the site of the vast majority of the legislators' work. Only four states—California, Florida, North Carolina, and Texas—provide their legislators with office space in the capitol. There are plans for similar space in Hawaii, New Mexico, and New Jersey. But most legislators improvise work-space in their hotel rooms or even at their legislative desks, or, if they live in or near the capital, use the facilities of their private business or occupation. In most legislatures, work-space for the activities even of committees and other official groups of legislators is at a premium, if it is available at all. The average committee is required to improvise its space from meeting to meeting. Quite commonly, private or closed meetings are held in a corner of the legislative chamber or in a hotel room, while public hearings are often conducted in the legislative chamber itself after full sessions, in hotel ballrooms, state office buildings, or elsewhere.

By almost any standard, the physical facilities in which all but a very few American state legislatures undertake their tasks are limited or even primitive. A modern business attempting to carry on under comparable circumstances would be thought hopelessly out of date.

LEGISLATIVE ADMINISTRATION AND HOUSEKEEPING

Like any complex organized enterprise a legislature needs a number of routine chores performed for it day by day and year by year. The agencies for performing elementary clerical and administrative tasks are today very much the same as those in the seventeenth and eighteenth century British Parliament, from which the American colonial assemblies copied. All legislative chambers have their private internal police force, so to speak, in the person of sergeants-at-arms.

In every chamber a chief clerk presides over a more or less numerous body of subordinate clerks who process the legislative papers, keep legislative records, and generally perform the mechanical functions associated with legislative operations. Clerical staffs may be more numerous today than a century ago, but their methods are not revolutionarily different. One is tempted to say merely that the ball-point has replaced the quill pen. Automated or computerized storage and retrieval of information, which by now is commonplace in many industries, is still unheard of in state legislative operations.

To the student or citizen accustomed to dealing with congressional operations, the record-keeping habits of most state legislatures would appear most unsatisfactory. Clerical effort was historically devoted almost entirely to the production of an archival record of past actions. Consequently, every legislative house today publishes a journal. In thirty-two states the journal is now published daily during sessions, and not merely after adjournment. But state legislative journals tend to be highly formal and skeletal records of events transpiring during a session. Roll-call votes are usually reported, as are rulings of the chair, but not verbatim transcripts or even summaries of debate. In many journals it is not recorded which members took the initiative to move passage, propose amendments, or otherwise perform their legislative functions. Still less complete records are maintained with respect to committee activities in state legislatures. Very few states print committee reports; fewer still print records of committee hearings. In many cases committee records are not even maintained in typed or raw note form.

Although some persons argue that more detailed journals would serve no useful purpose, except for historians and students of legislatures, it seems that being "on the record" would tend to keep individual legislators and the total legislature responsible to anyone who cared to inspect the record. It would also seem that printed committee reports and hearings might well be of inestimable value to legislators required to act on those reports or to be informed by those hearings.

Even more essential to the legislator in his daily work, it would seem, are copies of the bills with which he is supposed to deal. Even now about one-third of the American states do not provide legislators with printed copies of bills on which action is expected. Of these, some ten do not even provide mimeographed or any other form of copies of bills. Still fewer routinely print proposed amendments to pending bills. There is likewise considerable variation among legislatures in the character and quantity of information given legislatures about the status of bills, including information about the calendar or agenda for any given legislative day. Some states present each day a rather full list of what bills are to be brought to the floor of a chamber, what committees will hold hearings on what bills, and so on. Others provide only an end-of-the-day chalk-up on a blackboard in the chamber of likely business for the coming day, with at best a brief oral announcement on the floor of committee meetings or hearings.

In a number of respects, then, state legislators, even in states with the most advanced legislative plants, are forced to work with surprisingly limited facilities. As individuals, they rarely have even clerical assistance and almost never the kind of executive staff assistance which some of their work might seem to require. As a body, they frequently must work in physically inadequate surroundings, and without adequate information in the form of records and copies of the papers with which they are supposed to be dealing. At best, therefore, the modern American state legislature begins its work under certain handicaps.

The Organization of Legislative Production

Given the legislative manpower mobilized in the kind of surroundings and with the kind of facilities provided, how can or should the legislature go about its tasks? What routines, what procedures can or should it follow? The answers in any particular case will depend to some extent upon what kind of personnel and facilities are available. But inasmuch as the legislative function is fundamentally similar in many respects from one state to another, patterns or routines for certain basic phases of the legislative operation must be developed in every state.

LEGISLATIVE SESSIONS

State legislatures are in session much less frequently than the national legislatures of other countries, including the United States Congress. Indeed, only some fifteen states are without constitutional limitation on the length of either regular or special sessions, while another ten limit regular but not special sessions. The legislatures of the remaining twenty-five states are limited with respect to the length of both regular and special sessions. The limits on regular sessions run from as low as 40 calendar days to as high as 120 legislative and 195 calendar days; for special sessions, the limits run from 15 calendar days to 40 legislative and 60 calendar days.

Only nineteen states in 1964 had annual legislative sessions, and of these, nine had so-called regular sessions in odd years and budget sessions in even years (vice versa in Louisiana). Only seven of the nineteen having annual sessions did not have limits imposed on the length of sessions. The remaining thirty-one states had legislative sessions in odd years, except for Kentucky, Mississippi, and Virginia, where the legislatures met in even years.

Not all legislatures are empowered to call themselves into special session, and not all may determine what business they shall consider if so called. In fact, only five states vest full discretion for calling a special session with the legislature itself, and only another seven permit legislatures to call such sessions by special majorities or other special procedures. In most states the prerogative of convoking a special legislative session rests with the governor. In twelve states the legislature, once called into special session, has no control over the subjects with which it may deal. In another five states it has only limited control.

The practice of holding budget sessions in the "off years" is a response, primarily, to the desire to enable legislators to consider budgets on an annual rather than a biennial basis. It has been proposed in a similar vein that legislatures should adopt the practice of a "split session," whereby during the first half of a session bills might be introduced and committees activated; during the interim hearings would be held, and other preliminary legislative work accomplished; during the second half of the session no bills would be introduced and the legislature would presumably be free to concentrate fully on the hearings and bill consideration.

The budget session in alternate years is perhaps not a suitable analogy for justifying the proposed split session since the budgets in question are necessarily considered on a fixed schedule, whereas other policy matters do not necessarily come up by the calendar. To preclude introduction of bills during half a session, as proponents of the split session suggest, might actually have the effect of shortening the useful portion of the legislative session. On the other hand, to permit introduction of emergency legislation during the deliberative half of a split session might easily result in the same flow of legislation as before the split, through the fiction of labeling ordinary proposals "emergency" measures.

Nevertheless, relatively infrequent and short legislative sessions, and relative powerlessness to secure extra time through special sessions, make it extremely difficult for legislatures to cope with the enormous volume of business described in the preceding chapter. Although limitations on the legislature's capacity for action stem largely from state constitutional restrictions, it should not be assumed that formal change of constitutional limitations surrounding legislative sessions, even if that difficult process could be accomplished, would automatically produce the changes intended. As we have seen, the legislators actually recruited are in many instances men who can afford only a limited time away from their private occupations. It is not impossible, therefore, that existing patterns of legislative sessions, although originally shaped primarily by formal constitutional prescription, might be continued even without such prescriptions by force of habit or out of felt need on the part of present members.

LEGISLATIVE LEADERSHIP

As Malcolm Jewell has said in *The State Legislature: Politics and Practice*, "Nowhere do the realities of the legislative process differ more from the formal, legal framework than in the organizational structure." State legislatures have a formal hierarchy of officers superficially much like that found in the United States Congress, and most have a more or less formal hierarchy of party legislative officers much like congressional party organization. But, as we have seen earlier (Chapter 3 especially), legislative party balance varies from overwhelming one-party dominance in some states to close two-party competition in a few, and in two states—Minnesota and Nebraska—legislators are elected on a nonpartisan basis. Since no single factor is more critical in determining leadership structures than a state's party system, and since no factor permits a wider range of actualities to masquerade behind similar façades, one should not be too surprised by the bewildering variety of leadership structures among the fifty states. Even among states with somewhat comparable party systems, we find considerable variation in the realities of legislative organization. In this section we will point out a few of the critical kinds of decision making associated with legislative leadership, so that when examining a particular legislature, if we find who makes these decisions and how, we can say we have identified its particular leadership structure.

In principle, certain types of decision fall within the province of the presiding officer, the nominal chief officer of the house, in almost all legislative bodies. Nominally, at least, he determines the flow of discussion and debate on the floor by applying the rules adopted by the house for that purpose. Nominally, at least, in most states he makes important decisions before measures even come to floor debate, through his authority to assign members to committees, to appoint chairmen of committees, and to assign bills to one committee instead of another. Nominally, in most legislative bodies, the presiding officer is the elected agent of the members of the house. This is the case with all Speakers in our lower houses, although senates are usually presided over by a Lieutenant Governor elected on a statewide ballot. (Tennessee reverses the usual pattern by having the presiding officer whom its Senate elects become the Lieutenant Governor.)

The actualities of presiding officers' powers and functions, as well as the method of deciding who shall hold that office, may be quite different from the formal picture. In some instances the majority party effectively determines the choice because, as in Congress, the election in the house follows strict party lines after nominess are chosen in a party caucus or by some other party body. In others, the balloting in fact divides along the lines separating supporters of the governor from his opponents, cutting across party lines, with the governor in fact designating one contestant and some highly informal, factional type of group singling out another. Similarly, not many presiding officers manage debate and the flow of bills with the arbitrary power which formal rules often seem to allow them. Some follow closely the advice or orders of some agency of their party. Some are agents of the governor. Some rely on support from a group they organize in support of themselves (like the Speaker's Coalition in California).

But few Speakers in any of these cases wield the kind of unfettered influence that once led some Speakers of the United States House of Representatives to be called "Boss" and "Czar." Few really make appointments to committees except within bounds of traditional members' rights and titles to assignments; in only a few houses do they have significant discretion to assign bills arbitrarily to one committee instead of another; they can use the power of recognition to steer debates in directions they wish only in the fashion generally tolerated by their memberships; they can allow or ignore calls for roll-call votes, allow or disallow quorum calls, enforce time limits rigidly or loosely, only within the bounds of the specific legislative customs of their house.

Much the same holds true of other offices and agencies which comprise the leadership structure of a state legislature. The most important are those which have to do with the "steering" function, that is, the scheduling of legislative business. (We shall consider the committee system separately in a moment.) Almost every house has a steering, policy, rules, or some such committee formally charged with assigning bills to the appropriate calendars for floor action and, sometimes, for determining what rules shall govern consideration of them on the floor. In some instances these bodies do little more than hand down decisions made for them in a majority party steering committee or caucus. In others, they follow the lead of the governor or the majority floor leader. In still others, they operate as a more or less independent group acting in the name of the legislature alone. Needless to say, the determination of the agenda is a major decision in the legislative process. Careful inspection of the realities of the power to "steer," therefore, is likely to afford considerable insight into the structure of power in any given legislative body.

Whereas in Congress the informal structure of party leadership provides much of the animating force behind legislative decisions made by formal leadership, party leadership in most state legislatures tends to be much more fluid and less influential. There are party caucuses in many states, and majority party caucuses control many decisions of the kind described above, particularly in relatively small bodies like the New Jersey houses. In most houses, even when the minority is habitually a very small minority, there are majority and minority floor leaders, but their role in guiding the flow of debate and influencing decisions behind the scenes rarely approaches that of the party leaders in Congress. Indeed, many of them perform essentially clerical and housekeeping functions, keeping track of bills and debates, acting as information agencies for members, and so on, rather than exercising influence on members. Some of them are floor leaders for the governor, rather than for a party, and mobilize members of both parties much as a majority leader might mobilize his fellow partisans in Congress.

All in all, compared with the more familiar picture of leadership in the United States Congress, the picture of leadership in American state legislatures is often blurred and indistinct. In few state legislatures does the mobilization of legislative advocacy and opposition, brought about by party organization in the legislature, approach that achieved by party organization in Congress. In few does the formal leadership structure of presiding officers and steering committees approximate the complexity and fullness familiar to students of Congress. In many respects, the leadership structure appears to the rank-and-file state legislator to be an agency of the rank and file, or of the whole house, in a way that congressmen often say they would like to see but never do.

The picture may be incomplete and sketchy, but that is not to say that leadership in any legislature is indeterminate. Despite fluctuations in party fortunes and despite succession in office of different presiding officers, different floor leaders, and others, the pattern in any given state tends to remain relatively constant over long periods. Thus, if the office of presiding officer is found to be an agency or point of leverage for the governor in one session, it is likely to serve the same function every time the state-house majority is of the same party as the governor. If a Speaker is found to be a relatively "free" and impartial presiding officer, independent of party or gubernatorial control in any one year, the odds are his predecessors and successors will be found to be similarly independent. In other words, despite the enormous variation in power, influence, and style from one state legislature to another, there is yet remarkable constancy in the leadership structure, *i.e.*, in the institutional pattern, in any given house.

COMMITTEES AND COMMITTEE SYSTEMS

Although at first glance almost all state legislative committee systems appear to have been copied from Congress, there is in actual practice wide variation from state to state. During one recent biennium, for example, the number of standing committees of a chamber varied from none in Connecticut, which had only twenty-eight joint standing committees, to fifty in the Mississippi House. On the whole, standing committees are more numerous in state legislatures than in Congress since the latter was reorganized by the Legislative Reorganization Act of 1946.

Closely related to the number of committees, of course, is their size. Here again we find considerable range, not only between states but between committees within a state. Not long ago one state (Delaware) had exactly five members on each standing committee in both House and Senate, while at that same time House committees in the State of Washington varied in size from eleven to forty-one, and Vermont's legislature had joint committees ranging from as few as six members to as many as fifty-six.

The number and size of committees may help to limit or promote a legislature's ability to develop subject-matter specialists and to assign bills for consideration to committees comprised largely of legislators expert in the bill's subject matter. Committee jurisdictions in almost all cases in the states, just as in Congress, are defined in subject-matter terms—"Highways," "Finance," "Education," and so on. Yet a chamber having only three standing committees, as did the Maine Senate in recent years, will necessarily find a heterogeneous assortment of bills assigned to all of them. On the other hand, it can be argued that if extreme specialization accompanies the multiplication of committees, legislators in committee will rarely be considering a sufficiently broad range of bills to see clearly the over-all effect of any one bill before them. The number and size of committees will also affect the ability of the Speaker, or whoever effectively controls the assignment of bills to committee, to influence action on a bill by sending it to a committee which he knows to be sympathetic to the action he favors.

Some states have increasingly resorted to joint committees, composing members from both houses, as has Congress. But almost half the states in recent sessions have had no joint committees. It is usually argued that joint committees save time for citizens and legislators because testimony need be given in only one hearing, and that more useful information will probably be produced in one joint hearing than in two separate and presumably smaller-scale hearings.

Uniformity among committee systems appears greatest in the method of making committee and chairmanship appointments. Formally, the Speaker in all but five lower houses and the presiding officer (president pro tem.) in all but seventeen senates appoints members to committees. In a number of these latter seventeen chambers, members are selected by a senate committee on committees, or some other committee empowered to act as such. But, as we have just seen, the actuality of the appointing power may be quite different. Seniority rarely plays the role in state legislatures that it does in congressional committee assignments. Not only are members more often displaced from committees to which their seniority might seem to entitle them, but in some chambers chairmanships are given to minority party members. And, in the words of William J. Keefe and Morris S. Ogul, in *The American Legislative Process: Congress and the States,* "party, political, factional, and personal considerations often circumscribe the speaker's selections."

The significant question with respect to committee appointments, of course, is "who is advantaged and who is disadvantaged?" Are committees "stacked," either generally or variably from committee to committee, in favor of certain interests? It is often alleged that committees in Florida are "stacked" in favor of interests locally dubbed "pork-choppers." Equally common is the allegation that committees are "stacked" against rural interests.

Whether the number and size of committees, or the assignment of members to them, has any special consequence for the operation of a legislature, and whether or not anyone benefits specially from a given arrangement, will depend upon committee functions, powers, and practices. Public hearings, for example, play a much smaller role in state legislatures than in Congress. Hearings are required to be public in twenty states, and may be held in all. But fifteen states take no record of committee proceedings or hearings at all, and a number of others take only the sketchiest account. In some states committees rarely even meet, and when they do, rarely take any formal action. Unlike committee action in Congress, where committee recommendations are seldom rejected by the full house and matters seldom come before the house without prior committee action, committee action in most state legislatures is much less decisive.

While we must be alert to the variety of practices among the states and the specific import of practices in any particular state that concerns us, it is still fair to say that the general picture of state legislative committee systems shows them to be, on the average, more archaic in form, in terms of number, size, and description of their jurisdiction, as well as less influential in the legislative process than their congressional counterparts. Many things that Congress does in its committees, state legislatures do either on the floor in full session or not at all. It may be correct to say that state legislative committees have, on the whole, less power to bottle up, emasculate, or re-make legislative proposals than do congressional committees. It is also correct to say that many legislatures do not give bills the thorough scrutiny or give interested parties the opportunity to bring their views to bear on proposals which Congress expects of its committees.

STAFF ORGANIZATIONS FOR THE LEGISLATURE

We have seen that individual legislators generally get little staff assistance, that most legislatures are desperately short of committee working space, of facilities for reproducing and distributing copies of bills and amendments, and of other necessities. State legislative committees in only the rarest instances have staffs, counsels, and work forces like those of congressional committees. In one area, however, state legislatures have benefited from a "tooling up" which matches in scope and importance the changes made in Congress by the major reorganization acts. This is the development of permanent legislative service agencies.

Legislative reference services, the earliest form of these agencies, provided primarily a specialized collection of reference materials used by legislators in considering proposed legislation. They have become increasingly numerous since the first were established in Massachusetts and New York during the 1890s. The Wisconsin Legislative Reference Library, which was established in 1901 in close association with a state library commission and which provided "spot research" service to legislators on request, became a model for many later agencies of this type. Originally, the drafting of bills was one major function performed by the legislative reference service, which frequently displaced the office of attorney general as the chief agency for this purpose. But services attached to state libraries tended in time to concentrate more on research and less on bill drafting. In many states the latter job has been assumed by legislative councils.

The growth of legislative councils has without doubt been the most important development in this field. After the first was created by Kansas in 1933, some forty states instituted one form or another of a council. In general, the legislative council is a permanent, bipartisan, bicameral legislative research committee. It normally meets periodically between sessions, directs research into issues confronting the legislature, deliberates as a committee, and makes reports and recommendations to the legislature. Councils usually have full-time professional research staffs. Some councils may study only subjects assigned to them by formal resolution of the legislature, but most of them may undertake studies on their own initiative, and therefore can in some instances wield considerable influence over the legislative agenda for the coming session.

It was earlier feared that legislative councils might become "little legislatures," taking power from the total body. The fact that membership in them is exclusively legislative, save in Georgia, New Hampshire, South Carolina, and Utah, at first seemed to give some grounds for the fear. But most experts agree that this did not occur. Instead, legislative councils appear to have become major staff agencies of their legislatures, doing for them some of the kinds of research into technical feasibility, effects on interests, and other legislative considerations that the hyperactive committees do for the United States Congress.

The legislative council movement has been supplemented or broadened in recent years by efforts to expand the kinds of service rendered to the legislatures, whether by legislative councils themselves or by some other agency. In a significant report of 1963, called *Mr. President . . . Mr.*

Speaker . . . , the National Legislative Conference's Committee on Organization of Legislative Services called generally for increased staff services. Among the services usually considered appropriate for legislative councils or similar bodies to provide to the legislature are these: reference library facilities, bill drafting, statutory revision, legal counsel for legislators, preparation of bill and law summaries, recommendation of substantive legislative programs, preparation of research reports, "spot research," continuous study of state finances, budgetary review and analysis, and legislative post-audit. At the time the report was written, all these services were available to the legislature in only five states—Alaska, Florida, Louisiana, Michigan, and Pennsylvania, although in none of these states were all the services provided by any one agency. As the business of legislatures increases, it seems both necessary and inevitable that the provision of such staff services will also increase.

Deliberation and Decision

For most persons the term "legislative procedures" probably means rules by which a legislature handles business in plenary sessions on the floor—proposing, debating, and voting on measures. There is no question about the importance of such rules, but we must remember that they play their part within the context of legislative organization and practices. The actual effect of particular procedures and rules of debate and decision will in many cases be determined more by the realities of power and influence in these larger terms than by rules of order or similar formal enactments.

INITIAL STAGES IN THE LEGISLATIVE PROCESS

The gross outlines of the legislative process are almost identical in all states. As in Congress, measures may be introduced by any member who submits his proposal in a prescribed form to the clerk of the house. In some states joint sponsorship of measures is permitted; in others it is not. Although no formal provisions govern the process by which the sponsors write or acquire their draft proposal, its origins may in fact materially influence the fate of the proposal. Hastily or thoughtlessly concocted proposals stand much less chance of favorable action than bills thoroughly prepared with the aid of a bill-drafting or advisory agency.

More important, the fate of some bills is heavily influenced by their sponsors' legislative reputation, since on matters not directly affecting their major concerns busy legislators are usually quite willing to let themselves be guided by the judgment of colleagues whom they consider intelligent, informed, and reliable. Even more important, in most legislatures there is a tacit executive imprimatur on bills sponsored by the governor or administrative heads whom he backs, or on bills more or less formally adopted as part of a party legislative program, where parties perform that function. In some states such bills get formal advantages over others, something like the advantages given to Government bills in France and in some other countries. For example, at the request of the governor a bill may, when introduced, be exempted from time-consuming procedures or restrictions to which other bills are usually subject. Even without any formal advantages of this kind, bills having the status of "administration" or "party bills" may in fact be given priority over other measures throughout succeeding stages of the process.

In an effort to insure that measures have some chance for adequate consideration, as well as to cut down somewhat on the volume of legislative business, time limits for the introduction of bills are imposed in some states. In the Indiana House, for example, bills are not supposed to be introduced after the thirtieth day of the session. Less than ten states are without limitations of any kind in both houses. Where such limitations exist, however, there are usually special procedures for making exceptions to them, such as resolution by two-thirds vote, or unanimous consent.

About a dozen states seek to accomplish similar goals by permitting bills to be filed (introduced) before sessions formally open. In all states except Vermont and Wyoming, the normal bill-drafting service is available before sessions as well as during them. The proposal for "split sessions" represents another attempt to secure adequate time for consideration of measures on which the legislature must act.

DELIBERATION AND DEBATE

Formally, once a bill or resolution is properly introduced, the only requirement for it to become an authoritative action of the house where it is introduced is that it pass the house on three "readings," by whatever margin the rules call for, with a specified lapse of time between introduction and last reading. (In the Iowa House, the Maine Senate, and both Rhode Island chambers, only two readings are required.) Most commonly the requirement is that the separate readings be on separate days, but in most cases the three stages may be telescoped in emergencies, by special votes or special procedures, into less than three days. In actual practice, however, the three "readings" include processes more comprehensive and important than simple "reading" of the text of a bill, and, in fact, seldom include three actual readings of it. In most cases "first reading" comprises the Clerk's reciting the title of a bill or proposal and the number he has assigned to it. It is then referred to a committee for further action, as described earlier in this chapter.

As we have seen, the committee stage is significant, but not as much as in Congress. In a dozen or so states the power to pigeon-hole proposals has been taken from committees by requiring all committees to report on all bills referred to them. In many other states it is comparatively easy—by simple majority vote, for example—to force a bill out of a committee which refuses to act on it.

In most states, the committee stage is followed by debate and discussion of a measure on the floor. It is normally at this stage that amendments are proposed, and accepted or rejected. Before this happens, however, some agency must assign the bill to its place on the list of matters to be considered.

Assignment of bills on the calendars is performed in a variety of ways, but the agency actually making the decisions which fix the calendar will almost always include the most significant and powerful members of the body. In some houses there is a committee called "Calendar Committee," "Steering Committee," or some similar name, composed in some instances of committee chairmen, in others of the top legislative leadership. In other houses, the calendar is determined by the majority party caucus or some other party agency.

The agenda for floor action is generally much more simple in state legislatures than in the United States House of Representatives. In place of a number of different kinds of calendars ("Consent Calendar," "Union Calendar," and so on), there is frequently little more than a listing of bills one day for action the next.

Control of the agenda becomes most important as the end of a session approaches. The congressmen and the press have publicized the anguish of national legislators caught in the crush of end-of-session business, but the avalanche that buries state legislators in the closing weeks is, if that is possible, even more devastating. In many states it becomes impossible even to find bills, let alone secure action on them. It is at this point more than any other that the limited time, limited facilities, and limited institutional capacities of state legislatures combine with the thousands of proposed measures to bury legislature and legislators under mountains of paper.

Discussion and debate on the floor is more restricted than in Congress. Extended filibusters are practically impossible in all state legislative chambers, although during the closing days of a session monopoly of the floor for even a fraction of an hour may become an invaluable weapon. Almost everywhere debate can be ended by some familiar parliamentary tactic for cloture (*e.g.*, calling the previous question). Moreover, restrictions on the length and number of speeches on any one topic by any one member are almost universal, genuinely restrictive, generally observed and, if need be, enforced.

Informal rules do little to mitigate these restrictions. The 1957 study of four states mentioned earlier found that legislators not only strongly disapproved of "longwinded speeches," and "hogging the floor," but equally disapproved of legislators' speaking on subjects on which they are poorly informed or using the floor as a campaign platform to make speeches little relevant to issues at hand. On the other hand, the member's right to take part in proceedings on the same terms as his peers is a right stoutly upheld by all legislators, and sanctions cutting into that right are brought to bear only in the case of the gravest offenses against the legislative body. These practices viewed all together led one astute observer to call the state legislatures "bill-passing machines" instead of "deliberative bodies."

In any case, sooner in all state legislatures than in Congress, practically every bill arriving at the stage of debate and discussion is brought to a vote. It matters little whether this be "on second reading" or "on third reading." What counts is that there is an almost universal rule: debate is concentrated at only one of these times and it follows committee consideration or whatever other "staff" analysis the legislature might have available.

VOTING AND VOTING RULES

When it comes to the methods of making decisions during and at the end of debate, the hurdles are formally higher in state legislatures than in Congress. In more than thirty states final passage requires a constitutional majority or some closely approximate number—that is, a majority of the total membership, defined in one of several possible ways. Where such a requirement is found, absence or abstinence from voting is, in effect, a hostile vote.

State legislatures use fewer informal methods of voting than does Congress. Many states require roll-call votes on final passage, and almost all those not requiring roll calls make it relatively easy for a small minority (one-fifth of the members, or even two or three or five members) to demand that a roll call be taken. Neither teller votes (whereby members file by a "Yea" or a "Nay" teller to be counted) nor voting by division (*i.e.*, by members' physically separated into groups for counting) are familiar in state legislative bodies, inasmuch as few dissolve themselves into a committee-of-the-whole to expedite business, as does Congress. Voice votes may be taken on amendments clearly supported by heavy majorities, or on procedural matters of slight consequence. But for the most part, when it comes time to decide whether to adopt some amendment, to pass a bill, or to take any action that is either legislative in character or hotly contested, the normal method of voting is by call of the roll. Of course, this procedure is now quite expeditious in those thirty-five of the ninety-nine state legislative chambers equipped with electric roll-call machines.

As in Congress, the bicameral character of state legislatures, except in Nebraska, means that once a measure is passed in one house, that measure goes to the other house where it undergoes the same treatment all over again. As in Congress, so in most states, when two houses fail to agree on a measure a conference committee composed of members from each house is chosen to iron out differences, and the resulting compromise version is customarily accepted without further debate by both chambers.

As in national government, so in all states, bills finally passed in this way go to the executive for signature. Governors are in some states endowed with a veto power substantially greater than the president's, namely, the "item veto." Whereas a president signs or rejects a measure only as a whole, governors can in almost all states approve an appropriation bill over-all while vetoing specific items in it. In some states the same can be done to other types of bills as well. Moreover, while in many states a bill passed by the legislature automatically becomes law if the governor does not veto it within a specified time, in almost as many other states a bill dies if the governor does not sign it. In the case of vetoes and item vetoes, of course, it requires re-passage by an exceptional majority (two-thirds of the elected members is the most common requirement) for the legislature to pass the measure over the governor's veto.

This is perhaps the place to note one form of decision making found in many legislatures but not always understood by the general public. This is the fictional procedure for passing "local bills." The formal rules-of-order and by-laws rarely distinguish between the "general bill," which affects people and activities in a wide area or throughout the state (highway regulations, for example), and measures specifically regulating or referring to matters only within a particular county or district (like a regulation of the hunting season in a specifically named county). By invariably observed informal rules in many legislatures such local bills are decided entirely by the legislator or legislators from the affected district.

In such cases the legislative vote "passing" the measure is wholly fictional, in that no one but the interested member or members is even present in the hall when the matter is brought up, although if legally required the record may later report a vote that was never taken. Other stages in the legislative process for such bills are equally fictional. Where this kind of delegated authority on local matters prevails, however, there is usually found another strong informal rule of procedure. When members of a delegation do not agree unanimously on a local matter, the measure will not pass. It is also quite common to find that informal rules require that the measure bear the approval of a local unit of government (*e.g.*, city council) before the legislator is allowed the privilege of this autonomous local-bill procedure.

Institutional Modernization

Although it is often said that the American people do not trust their state legislatures, it does not follow that legislatures have been frequent targets of intensive reform efforts. Indeed, the paucity of ambitious proposals for institutional reform is rather startling in light of the common complaints about "Those Dinosaurs—Our State Legislators" (the title of an article by Thomas C. Desmond in the *New York Times*

Magazine, January 16, 1955). Dean Jefferson B. Fordham's trenchant comments on the institutional inadequacies of these bodies, in *The Legislative Institution,* afford one of the few comprehensive analyses of this kind available. Indeed, there have been no reform movements in the states comparable to the efforts on the national scene which led to the LaFollette-Monroney Legislative Reorganization Act of 1946, nor any prolonged battles over organization or procedure such as produced the "revolt against the Speaker" in Congress, culminating in the changes made in 1909-11. Consequently, there have been no broad-gauge state legislative reorganizations comparable to these changes in Congress.

DIAGNOSES, PRESCRIPTIONS, AND PANACEAS

The criticisms most commonly aimed at state legislatures include the charges that: (1) they are controlled by entrenched oligarchies who block the will of majorities; (2) power and authority is so fragmented and dispersed that, even if affairs are not oligarchically run, it is difficult to mobilize and maintain majorities which sustain themselves throughout the stages of the legislative process; (3) they waste time on petty and trivial matters; and (4) their operations are generally sloppy and inefficient. The precise evidence of these deficiencies is rarely presented, and even less often are suggestions made for specific steps which might correct them. But it seems clear that only the last of these common criticisms aims mainly at legislative organization and procedure.

Even so, the arguments advanced on behalf of one or another proposed legislative "reform" sometimes tend to make a relatively limited change sound like a cure for all the listed ills. The proposal to increase legislative pay, for instance, is sometimes justified with the hope that higher rewards will attract better men, who will not be inclined to wield power oligarchically, will be sensible enough to surmount inconveniences of a fragmented power system, will have vision enough to deal only with grave matters of the public interest, and will be able enough to improvise remedies for inefficiency and sloppy procedures. Lengthening the term of legislative office is frequently proposed on the same grounds, but not necessarily as a coordinate measure to be taken in conjunction with raising legislative pay. Some of the early crusaders in the legislative council movement also tended to urge its adoption as a panacea for all the ailments of the legislature.

For the most part, however, changes in legislative organization and procedure, where they have occurred at all, appear to have come piecemeal, in response to rather limited demands, expressed in low key and justified on what might be labeled "professional" grounds, rather than in response to comprehensive, strident reformist pleas. The introduction of electrical roll-call machines, the gradual improvements in facilities and procedures for the mechanical processing of legislative papers—filing, reproducing, distributing, and up-dating bills, etc.—are typical of the kinds of changes by which most legislatures have attempted to adjust to changing demands put upon them. In no states have there been major "reorganization fights" to reshuffle the powers and functions of legislative officers or to change the rules of discussion and debate. The tendency in some states to lengthen legislative sessions or to meet annually instead of biennially, in spite of the constrictive constitutional limits in this area, similarly has come normally through changing practices and not through formal revision of the whole system.

In all these instances, the lack of dramatic and comprehensive changes is to be explained not by opposition and uncooperativeness on the part of legislatures which refuse to reform themselves—as may be said to be the case with respect to reapportionment—but by the absence of sustained and intensive demand from either inside or outside the legislature. The changes that have occurred can in general be comprehended best as the product of the legislators' own efforts to improve the competence of their own legislatures.

CRITERIA FOR JUDGING LEGISLATIVE FUNCTIONING

The positive value of increasing professional expertise of legislative bodies should not be minimized. Competence in the performance of functions is the prime criterion for judging ability in any field. There is a danger, however, that a too narrow and technical definition of the legislators' functions may lead us to judge them by criteria which are either extraneous or very minor. Other things being equal, it is no doubt desirable that a legislature process each proposal for legislation as efficiently as possible. But it does all this only as a means of performing its really vital functions, which are political in nature.

The principal political functions of a legislature in a democratic system are, (1) to "represent" both the individuals, groups, and interests which make up the society and the communal interest of preserving and improving the aggregate society itself, and (2) to "legitimize" in the eyes of citizens the decisions made by government. So long as these functions rest in part with state legislatures, the most appropriate model by which to measure legislators is that of the citizen-amateur-politician-legislator, not the professionally and technically trained but politically detached craftsman of laws. Therefore, the standard for evaluating legislative institutions and processes should be: do they facilitate the performance of the representational and legitimizing functions by citizen-amateur-politician-legislators?

The division of labor through legislative organization and procedure must promote the most efficient acquisition and utilization of technical information and skills by legislators. Through staff research by legislative councils, committees, or whatever services are available, legislators must learn the technical consequences of choosing one type of highway system over another or one source of revenue over another. Legislators must learn through appropriate legal staff and counsel what statutory expressions and administrative arrangements will most efficiently secure the consequences they wish to promote and avoid those they do not want.

As Professor David Truman has convincingly indicated in his work on *The Governmental Process,* legislators need not only "technical" information and skill but "political" information and skill as well. "Political information" includes what legislators call the "effects of the bill"—what individuals or groups of citizens will be helped by the proposal? How? At whose expense? Does the distribution of benefits and disadvantages proposed unwittingly alter a distribution previously agreed on under some prior policy decision? The function of representation is the function by which legislators learn and make known to each other all such considerations.

The "effects" of a proposal include not only the specific benefits and disadvantages distributed by the proposal to various citizens and groups but, equally important, from the legislators' viewpoint, the probable reactions of citizens and groups to the proposed distribution. These include political reactions in the narrow sense of the word: will people change the way they vote or make campaign contributions as a result of the action taken? Even more, they comprise long-run reactions of citizens to their government and its policies, without direct reference to partisan or electoral politics. Will laws and policies enacted by the legislature be accepted as legitimate by living, feeling citizens? They will not be unless citizens have confidence that legislators have weighed carefully the "effects of the bill" before making it law and have done what they consider best in the public interest.

In the process of debate and deliberation everyone either explicitly or implicitly states what he thinks is the public interest. Needless to say, everyone tends to think that what he wants to do in the particular case is in the public interest. The legislature then decides what the public interest is on the basis of examining all these conceptions and inferring from them the "effects of the bill." To do this usually requires more than merely voting to accept one version or another as originally proposed, and more than merely parroting the expressed desires of constituents and other parties. It requires devising formulas to rationalize compromise on the part of competing interests, finding means for persuading parties to modify their views, and inventing wholly new proposals which subsume and extend the original competing proposals. By definition, the resulting formulation states what the public interest is in the matter under discussion. Because the end product is such an authoritative statement, it is likely to be accepted as legitimate by interested parties and the public at large.

The ultimate standard for judging proposals to change legislative organization and procedure in any respect is, therefore, two-fold: one, will the change improve performance of the legislature's legitimizing and representational functions? Two, will the change improve the legislature's ability (a) to recognize and receive all possible demands, complaints, anxieties, desires, or other stimuli to action from members of the citizen body; (b) to recognize the demands put upon government and public policy by the march of events even in advance of complaints and requests from citizen sources; (c) to receive and actively solicit both technical and politcal intelligence about the demands and the policies proposed to meet them; and (d) through deliberation and debate, both formally and in every other stage of the legislative process, to formulate the most "effective" decision to satisfy both the technical and the political needs involved?

The task thus described is never completed. Legislative organization and procedure, ideally, are stable patterns of behavior which permit the legislature continuously to perform its two principal functions of representing people, groups, and communities, and of legitimizing decisions in the name of the public interest.

Alexander Heard

6

Reform: Limits and Opportunities

American state legislatures have changed much since the formation of the Union. The early state constitutions converted colonial assemblies into legislative bodies intended to protect against an executive tyranny the colonists had grown to fear. The resulting large powers and high public favor that early legislatures enjoyed were replaced as the conduct of the legislatures themselves destroyed public confidence. The legislatures often fell victim to the selfish ambitions of their own members and to pressures by outside interests.

In addition, as the suffrage broadened, segments of the population not hitherto influential gave voice to their demands through representatives in the state assemblies. Established orders felt threatened. Out of a variety of motives, the revised state constitutions adopted after the Civil War placed a wide range of restrictions on the legislatures.

These bodies continue today shackled by limited powers and by constitutional specifications that fix, often in startling detail, how a legislature must go about its business. The legislatures, moreover, even when they have had the power to make changes, have frequently through inaction left themselves burdened by obsolete features of organization and procedure. Under heavy handicaps, they perform essential governmental functions amidst enormous political changes, while other institutions of government have acquired increasingly significant roles. Yet, with all this, state legislatures remain critically important in the American governmental system and can become even more important as the nation's many-dimensional political structure adjusts to the altering situation in the decades ahead.

Democratic government is recurringly challenged to marshal sufficient on state legislatures imposed by the context in which they operate. Social and economic interests shape importantly the issues to be resolved and the alliances among the contestants for political power. The structures of power within the party system as well as constitutional provisions limit what legislatures can do of their own will to make themselves more effective. Heavy heritages of custom deeply influence each legislative body in its daily tasks and in its willingness and ability to change its ways. Significant changes in state legislatures, in other words, will stem from influences outside as well as inside these bodies.

Democratic government is recurringly challenged to marshal sufficient effective power to accomplish needed public purposes while holding those exercising this power effectively responsible. These are the goals to which, in the end, measures of reform and improvement are merely means.

Two fundamental changes from the outside have given new significance to what can be accomplished by constitutional and statutory enactments. Compulsory reapportionment promises to make state legislative assemblies more accurate reflections of political interests in the nation than they have ever been before. Moreover, two-party politics is emerging in many areas previously dominated by either Democrats or Republicans. The causes lie outside the legislatures, but these developments offer the prospect that more effective party (and factional) organization will develop within some legislative chambers. Where this occurs, a legislature will find itself better positioned to perform its political functions—which is to say its basic legislative functions—and will find that improvements it can effect in its own internal operations will take on greater meaning.

The Future Importance of State Legislatures

United States senators were once elected by state legislatures. This and other functions made these bodies at times more a focus of attention for special interests than any other organ of government— federal, state, or local. That the relative significance of state legislative functions has declined should not obscure the continuing vitality of these bodies nor the present importance of the tasks they perform.

The government of the United States is effected through a mass of diverse and specialized channels. Needs are expressed, expertness applied, decisions made, and sanctions imposed via an intricate set of political and regulatory systems. The whole of this government is comprised of several "levels" and the relations among them, of several "branches" and the mixed agencies they have spawned, of numerous "functions" of government and kinds of public power, reaching in our time directly or indirectly to virtually everything we do. This governmental system *as a whole* accommodates to national changes. How the processes of accommodation involve and use a particular segment of government at a particular time depends on a large complex of forces, some perceptible, even manageable, others hidden or uncontrollable. The part that state legislatures will play in the future will necessarily depend to some extent on how well they are technically equipped to do specified things. Their past and present central responsibilities, however, are more telling indicators of their future significance in the American governmental system than the prospects that particular operational improvements will be made. The assured future importance of state legislatures emphasizes the significance of whatever improvements can be made in state legislative processes.

Thousands of bills are enacted into law by state legislatures every two years. They classify the crimes of murder and prescribe the punishment for each. They regulate conditions of private contracts and how recovery for a breach can be sought. They define a multitude of rights and responsibilities of organizations and individuals under the conditions of close living that characterize urban, industrial society. In a time of affirmative government, when government reaches out to do what has not been done before, or not been done before by public means, state legislatures are often decisive in determining whether, or how well, something shall be done. In the maze of governmental controls that result, state legislators find themselves in the demanding, if unwanted, role of special pleader for affected citizens. They influence the choice of personnel in other sectors of state government, sometimes actually electing them. They oversee with differing degrees of penetration the activities of state administrative agencies. They often have a general influence in state government much beyond their formal duties as legislators.

In the dynamic society of the United States, the state legislature is often the forum where new needs are expressed and innovation advocated. Illustrations have been given in this volume of pioneering activities that have later influenced the development of policy in other states and in the federal government. State legislatures have usually responded to the tides of need in society, often imperfectly, but sometimes swiftly and sensitively.

The role of the states in education, if nothing else, makes the state legislature a crucial organ of government in our future. The character of the primary and secondary school systems of the country, and increasingly of the college and university systems, is determined importantly by the policies and appropriations of state legislatures. Federal funds for education, especially higher education, increased after 1957 and surged upward particularly in 1965. These funds, however, were usually specialized in character, designed to aid specified groups or to encourage activities, like medical research, deemed by Congress important to the national interest. Deeper involvement by federal agencies in education notwithstanding, state legislatures seem destined to continue to control the bulk of public money going into educational instruction at all levels. As the interconnection of education with all aspects of a state's life continues to increase, the significance of legislative actions and attitudes in educational matters will also continue to rise. In all sorts of allied spheres, the arts for example, state legislative attitudes will also be important.

Avenues to Change

In these circumstances, the inadequacies of state legislatures made evident in this volume command attention. The authors have made it clear that political effectiveness does not always equate exactly to decorum in political behavior nor to superficial logic in legislative procedure. As with our presidential nominating conventions, the solid political achievements of American state legislatures are sometimes obscured by the blare and bluster of the political system. Nonetheless, much can be done to enhance the political effectiveness of state legislatures. Many improvements can be made by state legislatures themselves if they have the will to do so. State constitutional revision is required in some cases. Other changes depend on a different organization of party or factional political power if coherence in legislative programs, or effectiveness in legislative and state government leadership, is to be achieved. The avenues to state legislative reform are several and various.

The operating characteristics of legislative bodies, whatever their procedural and organizational features, are greatly influenced by the location of political power and how it is exercised. The location and exercise of political power, moreover, vary with the structure and processes of party organization outside the legislature, and with the activities and power of social and economic interest groups outside the parties.

Most prescriptions for state legislative improvement have been confined to changes in the legal powers, organization, and procedures of legislatures. The differing political context from one state to another, and the imponderable obstacles to effecting basic changes in this context, have understandably led those intent upon improvement to confine their proposals to concrete measures subject to legal action. The lack of systematic, comparable information, even in 1966, about political systems and factional and party behavior within individual states, is part of the difficulty. Moreover, given the differences known to exist from state to state, it has been difficult to generalize about the effects of procedural and structural changes on the distribution of political power within legislatures. The development of competitive politics in areas of previously low competition and the new apportionments are significant in themselves. They may have a further significance, however, if in the future they produce a climate of legislative operations in which specified procedural and organizational changes have more certain effects, and consequently greater significance, than previously.

The contributors to this volume have made clear that some features of state legislative behavior are beyond the reach of revisions that are usually advocated by champions of state legislative reform. These boundary conditions, although present, ought not to deter those who are intent on improving the quality of American political life. Many changes are necessary if state legislatures, and consequently state governments, are to perform more effectively. These changes by themselves may not be sufficient to accomplish all desired results, but they are necessary steps. The revision of state legislatures is related to the entire question of state constitutional reform and to the future effectiveness of state governments within the federal system. Viewing state legislatures in a large realistic context should not blind anyone, however, to the importance of steps that could be taken by more immediate action. The cumulative effect of a series of individual changes designed to improve the daily efficiency and annual effectiveness of state legislatures can be great, perhaps greater than easily predicted.

The Battalions of Reform

In early 1966 the press carried a release that began: "State Legislators from around the United States plan to establish a center to help them improve their methods of operation." The story explained that the executive committee of the National Conference of State Legislative Leaders, an organization of legislators from thirty-five states under the chairmanship of California's Speaker Jesse M. Unruh, had voted to cosponsor a legislative service center at the Eagleton Institute of Politics of Rutgers University of New Jersey.

Mr. Unruh is perhaps the most prominent state legislator in the United States. His California legislature has perhaps done more to improve its capacity to meet the extraordinary problems it faces than has any other. Mr. Unruh was reported as saying there was a national awareness of the ineptitude of state legislatures. In a competitive mood that those familiar with California state politics will understand, he ruefully observed that state legislatures are being outshone by the executive branches in their states.

This announcement was but one of several signs that influential forces in the nation were directing their attention to the plight of state legislatures.

The Carnegie Corporation had already made a grant to the Eagleton Institute for a three-year series of seminars directed toward sparking the self-improvement effort. That Institute had issued a report in 1963 commissioned by the New Jersey legislature that carried detailed proposals for legislative improvement. The Ford Foundation had made a five-year grant to the National Municipal League for a multi-pronged investigation of "the constitutional barriers, outdated practices and other factors which interfere with the effectiveness of legislatures." Former Governor John Anderson of Kansas headed the staff of another organization, the Citizens Conference on State Legislatures, with offices in Kansas City. The Conference, helped by donations from The Ford Foundation and the

Carnegie Corporation, and with businessmen in support, hoped to build public support for the reform of state legislatures. The American Political Science Association launched a set of fellowship programs designed to encourage the study and better staffing of these bodies.

These and other efforts were developed as supplements to the continuing activities of the National Municipal League and the Council of State Governments. The National Municipal League has tackled the problem of constitutional reform through its *Model State Constitution* and related publications. The National Legislative Conference, an association of state legislators and heads of legislative reference services for which the Council provides staff services, has for several years addressed itself to legislative reform. It has proposed alterations in legislative organization and procedure as well as in the services that have been developed to assist state legislatures. The National Legislative Conference issued a report with recommendations in 1961 called *American State Legislatures in Mid-Twentieth Century* and another in 1963 called *Mr. President . . . Mr. Speaker.*

Models for Change

The *Model State Constitution* gives preference to a unicameral legislature, although it provides a bicameral alternative. It vests the legislative power of the state in the legislature. It provides that the state budget, which requires legislative approval, shall embrace all anticipated expenditures, and earmarking of funds from specified sources is prohibited except where required by the federal government. Furthermore, after providing for the number of houses, the basis of apportionment, and terms and qualifications of legislators, it leaves other aspects of legislative operations to statutory or other regulation.

These proposals suggest well the constitutional base that many students of state legislatures consider necessary to provide the flexibility of operation and concentration of legislative authority required of state legislatures in the future. Within this framework, specific objectives can be set forth that constitute something of a model with which individual legislative bodies can be compared.

Donald G. Herzberg, Director of the Eagleton Institute, calls state legislatures the "emerging nations" of American politics. He groups the changes he sees needed in most of them under six headings. The "six s's" call for improved staff, services, space, salaries, sessions, and spirit. Measures that would bring the desired improvements have been formulated in various states over the years and have taken forms conditioned by the features of the individual states for which they were designed. Perhaps the most useful way to lay out the most generally applicable concrete proposals for change is to summarize the principal recommendations of the National Legislative Conference. They were offered first in 1961 and re-endorsed in 1964. That such proposals as these are not equally applicable to all states, and are limited in the effects they can accomplish, will be clear from the discussion of organization and procedures in Chapter 5. They constitute, nonetheless, a check list to be considered by those concerned with the effectiveness of American government.

1. *Legislative-Executive relations.* Legislatures should exercise fully their inherent powers toward re-establishing greater independence from the executive branch. They should establish procedures and staff facilities to assure effective legislative participation in matters such as pre-session evolution of public policy, pre-session preparation of legislative programs, appropriation of public funds, auditing their expenditure, and reviewing the uses made by administrative agencies of the delegated power to issue and enforce rules and regulations.

2. *Sessions.* Undue limitations and restrictions upon the length and subject matter of legislative sessions should be removed.

3. *Terms.* A term of four years in at least one house, with staggered terms for legislators, is cited as consistent with the objective of establishing legislative terms that assure effective responsibility to the voters and at the same time provide desirable continuity in legislative experience.

4. *Compensation.* Improved salary and expense policies are urged, with flat salaries and adequate reimbursement of necessary expenses rather than per diem allowances, toward the objective of permitting and encouraging competent persons to undertake increasingly important and time-consuming legislative duties. The amounts should be fixed by statute rather than by the constitution.

5. *Employees.* Full-time legislative employees should be appointed on merit. The tenure of technical and professional personnel whose work does not involve "partisan" activities should be determined by competence and not party control. The conditions of employment of legislative employees should be no less advantageous than those of employees in the executive and judicial departments.

6. *Committees.* In many states committees should be reduced in number. They should be organized with due regard to related subject matter, equalization of work load, cooperation between the houses, and reduction of undue burdens on individual members. Provision should be made for effective public hearings on major bills and the desirability of executive sessions, where necessary, should be emphasized.

7. *Legislation.* Some states should consider limiting by rule the period when new bills may be introduced. States where bulk of bills has been a problem should consider authorizing and encouraging the drafting, filing, and printing of bills before the opening of the session.

Where annual sessions are held unrestricted as to subject matter, consideration should be given to a system of carrying over bills on calendar from the first to subsequent sessions of the same legislature, both to expedite the legislative process and to reduce printing costs.

All bills and important amendments introduced should be printed prior to public hearings on them and before consideration by the legislature, and whenever possible they should be inspected before printing by bill drafters or revision clerks. Editorial review and appraisal of final enactments by competent staff should be provided much more widely than at present as a means of detecting errors and conflicts, prior to transmittal to the governor.

Adequate provision should be made for printing new laws and making them generally available at the earliest possible time after final enactment and before they become effective. If the volume of session laws cannot be thus available, new laws, adequately indexed, should be reproduced in some alternate form such as "slip laws" or "advance sheets."

8. *Modern equipment.* Legislatures should explore the wide range of electronic and other technological devices now available with an eye to their use in various aspects of the legislative process, *e.g.*, roll-call voting, reproduction of legislative measures, preparation of journals, recording of hearings and debates.

9. *Finance.* A legislature should provide itself with an adequate operating budget over which it has exclusive control and responsibility.

10. *Facilities.* Adequate office space should be provided legislators.

11. *Orientation.* All states should arrange orientation programs for new legislators to familiarize them with the legislative process and with the tools they have to work with.

12. *Local and special legislation.* In order that the legislature may devote its attention to formulating major public policy—general, optional, or home rule legislation should be enacted as substitutes for special legislation affecting cities, counties, and other political subdivisions of the states, particularly in matters of purely local concern. Consideration and settlement of claims against the state should be delegated to judicial or administrative agencies.

In addition to these proposals, the National Legislative Conference in 1963 issued a report containing an elaborate set of recommendations to improve the administrative, fiscal, legal, research, and other services available to legislatures and individual legislators, proposals alluded to in Chapter 5.

The Larger Tasks

Pragmatic proposals like these are largely designed to attack immediate operating problems. They constitute feasible steps toward maintaining state legislatures as viable parts of the existing governmental system. They do not pretend to do more.

Much more, of course, is involved in the larger tasks of creating government in the United States adequate to the nation's needs. The evolving character of the party system, general attitudes toward political careers, success in supplying and regulating campaign expenditures, the nature of the public policy questions created by a rapidly changing society, and other factors that reach to the roots of power and consensus will in the long run largely determine the role of state legislatures, and of the state governments to which they belong.

Education of the citizenry to the opportunities and responsibilities of state government is itself an important contribution to the development and maintenance of an effective governmental system. Attention to legislative reform, therefore, not only serves the useful purposes to be achieved by individual remedial measures. It helps also to focus attention upon the deeper forces that mold state governments and their legislatures, and with which the nation must contend in making democracy work.

Appendix

Characteristics of Legislatures

State	Constitutional Limit on Size S	H	Terms of Members S	H	Sessions Annual or Biennial[1]	Constitutional Limit on Length[2]	Special Sessions Legis. May Call[4]	Legis. May Determine Subject[4]	Number of Committees S	H	Joint	Committees Appointed by[3] S	H
Alabama	35	106	4	4	B	36L	N	Y	30	19	0	Pr	Sp
Alaska	20	40	4	2	A	None	Y	Y	9	9	0	Comm.	Comm.
Arizona	28	80	2	2	A	P—63C	Y	Y	21	21	0	Pr	Sp
Arkansas	35	100	4	2	B	60C	N	Y	25	26	1	Pr	Sp
California	40	80	4	2	A-Bud	120W	N	N	21	26	4	Comm.	Sp
Colorado	39	65	4	2	A-Bud	P—160C	N	N	20	17	1	Senate	Sp
Connecticut	36	294	2	2	B	150C	Y	Y	0	0	28	PrPT	Sp
Delaware	21	35	4	2	A-Bud	90L	N	Y	22	26	1	PrPT	Sp
Florida	45	112	4	2	B	60C	Y	Y	45	51	0	Pr	Sp
Georgia	54	205	2	2	A	45C	Y	Y	18	24	0	Pr	Sp
Hawaii	25	51	4	2	A-Bud	60W	N	Y	18	21	0	Pr	Sp
Idaho	44	79	2	2	B	P—60C	N	N	14	15	0	Pr	Sp
Illinois	58	177	4	2	B	None	N	N	25	26	0	Comm.	Sp
Indiana	50	100	4	2	B	61C	N	Y	29	28	0	PrPT	Sp
Iowa	50	108	4	2	B	None	N	Y	30	42	0	Pr	Sp
Kansas	40	125	4	2	A-Bud	P—90L	N	Y	31	45	1	Comm.	Sp
Kentucky	38	100	4	2	B	60L	N	N	37	45	1	Comm.	Comm.

1. A—Annual, B—Biennial, B-Bud—Every second annual session devoted to budget.
2. L—Legislative days, C—Calendar days, W—Weekdays, P—Limit is number of days for which legislators may be paid. Days shown are for length of regular sessions only, excluding lengths of budget sessions. Provisions such as power of legislature or governor to extend sessions are excluded.
3. Pr—President, PrPT—President Pro Tem, Sp—Speaker, Comm.—Committee.
4. N—No; Y—Yes.
Source: *Book of the States, 1964-65* (Chicago: Council of State Governments, 1964), pp. 43-51. Data are applicable to 1962 and 1963 sessions.

Characteristics of Legislatures (continued)

State	Constitutional Limit on Size		Terms of Members		Sessions		Special Sessions		Number of Committees			Committees Appointed by[3]	
	S	H	S	H	Annual or Biennial[1]	Constitutional Limit on Length[2]	Legis. May Call[4]	Legis. May Determine Subject[4]	S	H	Joint	S	H
Louisiana	39	105	4	4	A-Bud	60C	Y	Y	18	17	0	Pr	Sp
Maine	34	151	2	2	B	None	N	Y	3	6	26	Pr	Sp
Maryland	29	142	4	4	A-Bud	90	N	Y	16	15	3	Pr	Sp
Massachusetts	40	240	2	2	A	None	Y	Y	4	6	31	Pr	Sp
Michigan	38	110	4	2	A	None	N	N	21	48	0	Comm.	Sp
Minnesota	67	135	4	2	B	120L	N	Y	23	36	0	Comm.	Sp
Mississippi	52	122	4	4	B	None	N	N	46	50	5	Pr	Sp
Missouri	34	163	4	2	B	195C	N	N	28	45	2	PrPT	Sp
Montana	56	94	4	2	B	60C	N	N	23	18	0	Comm.	Sp
Nebraska	43	—	4	—	B	None	Y	N	14	—	—	Comm.	—
Nevada	17	37	4	2	B	P-60C	N	N	19	22	0	Pr	Sp
N. Hampshire	24	400	2	2	B	P-90L	Y	Y	18	24	1	Pr	Sp
N. Jersey	21	60	4	2	A	None	Y	Y	16	16	4	Pr	Sp
N. Mexico	32	77	4	2	B	60C	Y	Y	7	16	0	Comm.	Sp
N. York	58	150	2	2	A	None	N	N	28	36	0	PrPT	Sp
N. Carolina	50	120	2	2	B	P-120C	N	Y	34	46	4	Pr	Sp
N. Dakota	49	109	4	2	B	60L	N	Y	11	14	0	Comm.	Sp

1. A—Annual, B—Biennial, B-Bud—Every second annual session devoted to budget.
2. L—Legislative days, C—Calendar days, W—Weekdays, P—Limit is number of days for which legislators may be paid. Days shown are for length of regular sessions only, excluding lengths of budget sessions. Provisions such as power of legislature or governor to extend sessions are excluded.
3. Pr—President, PrPT—President Pro Tem., Sp—Speaker, Comm.—Committee.
4. N—No; Y—Yes.

Source: *Book of the States, 1964-65* (Chicago: Council of State Governments, 1964), pp. 43-51. Data are applicable to 1962 and 1963 sessions.

Characteristics of Legislatures (continued)

State	Constitutional Limit on Size		Terms of Members		Sessions		Special Sessions		Number of Committees			Committees Appointed by[3]	
	S	H	S	H	Annual or Biennial[1]	Constitutional Limit on Length[2]	Legis. May Call[4]	Legis. May Determine Subject[4]	S	H	Joint	S	H
Ohio	33	137	4	2	B	None	N	N	13	21	0	PrPT	Sp
Oklahoma	44	109	4	2	B	None	N	N	34	39	0	Senate	Sp
Oregon	30	60	4	2	B	None	N	Y	20	20	1	Pr	Sp
Pennsylvania	50	210	4	2	A-Bud	None	N	N	21	30	0	PrPT	Sp
Rhode Island	46	100	2	2	A	P—60L	N	N	17	15	1	Senate	Sp
S. Carolina	46	124	4	2	A	None	N	Y	25	8	5	Senate	Sp
S. Dakota	35	75	2	2	A	45L	N	Y	16	23	0	Pr	Sp
Tennessee	33	99	2	2	B	P—75C	N	N	17	17	0	Sp	Sp
Texas	31	150	4	2	B	140C	N	N	24	43	1	Pr	Sp
Utah	27	69	4	2	B	60C	N	N	14	16	1	Pr	Sp
Vermont	30	246	2	2	B	None	N	Y	18	19	3	Comm.	Sp
Virginia	40	100	4	2	B	P—60C	Y	Y	21	34	3	Senate	Sp
Washington	49	99	4	2	B	60C	N	Y	20	21	0	Pr	Sp
West Virginia	34	106	4	2	A-Bud	60C	Y	N	28	24	4	Pr	Sp
Wisconsin	33	100	4	2	B	None	N	N	11	23	5	Comm.	Sp
Wyoming	25	61	4	2	B	40C	N	Y	16	18	1	Pr	Sp

1. A—Annual, B—Biennial, B-Bud—Every second annual session devoted to budget.
2. L—Legislative days, C—Calendar days. W—Weekdays, P—Limit is number of days for which legislators may be paid. Days shown are for length of regular sessions only, excluding lengths of budget sessions. Provisions such as power of legislature or governor to extend sessions are excluded.
3. Pr—President, PrPT—President Pro Tem, Sp—Speaker, Comm.—Committee.
4. N—No; Y—Yes.
Source: *Book of the States, 1964-65* (Chicago: Council of State Governments, 1964), pp. 43-51. Data are applicable to 1962 and 1963 sessions.

Bibliography

Abernethy, Byron R., *Constitutional Limitations on the Legislature.* Lawrence: University of Kansas Governmental Research Center, 1959.

Abrams, Richard M., *Conservatism in a Progressive Era.* Cambridge: Harvard University Press, 1964.

Alexander, Herbert E., *Regulation of Political Finance.* Berkeley: Institute of Governmental Studies, and Princeton: Citizens' Research Foundation, 1966.

Balmer, Donald G., *Financing State Senate Compaigns: Multnomah County, Oregon, 1964.* Princeton: Citizens' Research Foundation, 1966.

Barber, James D., *The Lawmakers: Recruitment and Adaptation to Legislative Life.* New Haven: Yale University Press, 1965.

The Book of the States, The Council of State Governments, Chicago, biennial.

Buchanan, William, *Legislative Partisanship: The Deviant Case of California.* Los Angeles: University of California Press, 1963.

Census of Governments, U.S. Census Bureau, Washington, D. C., published at five-year intervals since 1952.

Compendium of State Government Finances, U.S. Census Bureau, Washington, D. C., annual.

Congress and the Nation, 1945-1964, Congressional Quarterly Service, Inc., Washington, D. C., 1965, pp. 1397-1400.

David, Paul T., and Ralph Eisenberg, *Devaluation of the Urban and Suburban Vote,* 2 Vols. Charlottesville: University of Virginia Bureau of Public Administration, 1961-62.

de Grazia, Alfred, *Apportionment and Representative Government.* Washington, D. C., Frederick A. Praeger, 1963.

Derge, David R., "The Lawyer as Decision-Maker in the American State Legislature," *Journal of Politics,* Vol. 21, 1959, pp. 408-33.

Derge, David R., "The Lawyer in the Indiana General Assembly," *Midwest Journal of Political Science,* Vol. 6, pp. 19-53.

Dixon, Robert G., Jr., "Congress and Reapportionment: Issues and Opportunities," *The George Washington University American Assembly Report on The Congress and America's Future.* Washington, D. C., The George Washington University, 1965, pp. 6-12.

Eagleton Institute of Politics, *The New Jersey Legislature,* New Brunswick, 1963.

Eastern, David, *A Systems Analysis of Political Life.* New York: John Wiley & Sons, Inc., 1965.

Epstein, Leon D., *Politics in Wisconsin.* Madison: University of Wisconsin Press, 1958.

Eulau, Heinz, and John D. Sprague, *Lawyers in Politics.* Indianapolis: Bobbs-Merrill Co., Inc., 1964.

Flinn, Thomas A., "Party Responsibility in the States: Some Causal Factors," *American Political Science Review,* Vol. 58, 1964, pp. 60-71.

Fiscal Services for State Legislatures, The Council of State Governments, Chicago, 1961.

Fisher, Glen W., "Determinants of State and Local Government Expenditures, a Preliminary Analysis," *National Tax Journal,* Vol. 14, 1961, pp. 349-55.

Garceau, Oliver, and Corinne Silverman, "A Pressure Group and the Pressured," *American Political Science Review,* Vol. 48, 1954, pp. 672-91.

Hacker, Andrew, "Pressure Politics in Pennsylvania," in *The Uses of Power,* ed. Alan F. Westin. New York: Harcourt, Brace & World, Inc., 1962, pp. 323-76.

Hamilton, H. D., ed., *Legislative Apportionment, Key to Power.* New York: Harper and Row Publishers, Inc., 1964.

Havard, William C., and Loren P. Beth, *The Politics of Mis-Representation: Rural-Urban Conflict in the Florida Legislature.* Baton Rouge: Louisiana State University Press, 1962.

Heard, Alexander, *The Costs of Democracy.* Chapel Hill: University of North Carolina Press, 1960.

Hurst, James Willard, *The Growth of American Law: The Law Makers.* Boston: Little, Brown & Co., 1950.

Hyneman, Charles S., "Tenure and Turnover of Legislative Personnel," *Annals of the American Academy of Political and Social Science,* Vol. 195, 1935, pp. 21-31.

Jacob, Herbert, and Kenneth N. Vines, eds., *Politics in the American States.* Boston: Little, Brown & Co., 1965.

Jewell, Malcolm E., *The State Legislature: Politics and Practice.* New York: Random House, 1962.

Jewell, Malcolm E., ed., *The Politics of Reapportionment.* New York: Atherton Press, 1962.

Keefe, William J., and Morris S. Ogul, *The American Legislative Process: Congress and the States.* Englewood Cliffs, N. J.: Prentice-Hall, Inc., 1964.

Keefe, William J., "Comparative Study of the Role of Political Parties in State Leglislatures," *Western Political Quarterly,* Vol. 9, 1956, pp. 726-42.

Key, V. O., Jr., *American State Politics: An Introduction.* New York: Alfred A. Knopf, Inc., 1956.

Key, V. O., Jr., *Southern Politics in State and Nation.* New York: Alfred A. Knopf, Inc., 1949.

Lockard, Duane, *New England State Politics.* Princeton: Princeton University Press, 1959.

Lockard, Duane, *The Politics of State and Local Government.* New York: The Macmillan Co., 1963.

Miller, Warren E., and Donald E. Stokes, "Constituency Influence in Congress," *American Political Science Review,* Vol. 57, 1963, pp. 45-66.

Model State Constitution, (6th ed.). New York: National Municipal League, 1963.

Morris, Willie, "Legislating in Texas," *Commentary,* Vol. 38, 1964, pp. 40-46.

National Legislative Conference, *American State Legislatures in Mid-Twentieth Century.* Chicago: Council of State Governments, 1965.

National Legislative Conference, *Mr. President . . . Mr. Speaker. . . .* Chicago: Council of State Governments, 1963.

Patterson, Samuel C., "Dimensions of Voting Behavior in a One-Party State Legislature," *Public Opinion Quarterly,* Vol. 26, 1962, pp. 185-200.

Penniman, Clara, "The Politics of Taxation," in *Politics in the American States,* eds. Herbert Jacob and Kenneth N. Vines. Boston: Little, Brown & Co., 1965, pp. 299-306.

Ransone, Coleman B., Jr., "Political Leadership in the Governor's Office," *Journal of Politics*, Vol. 26, 1964, pp. 197-220.

Robinson, James, and Richard Dawson, "Inter-Party Competition, Economic Variables, and Welfare Policies in the American States," *Journal of Politics,* Vol. 25, 1963, pp. 265-89.

Rogow, Arnold A., and Harold D. Lasswell, *Power, Corruption, and Rectitude.* Englewood Cliffs, N. J.: Prentice-Hall, Inc., 1963.

Sacks, Seymour, and Robert Harris, "Determinants of State and Local Government Expenditures and Intergovernmental Flow of Funds," *National Tax Journal*, Vol. 17, 1964, pp. 75-85.

Schlesinger, Joseph A., "The Politics of the Executive," in *Politics in the American States,* eds. Herbert Jacob and Kenneth N. Vines. Boston: Little, Brown & Co., 1965, pp. 217-32.

Schubert, Glendon A., *Reapportionment.* New York: Charles Scribner's Sons, 1965.

Shadoan, Arlene T., *Preparation, Review, and Execution of the State Operating Budget.* Lexington: University of Kentucky Bureau of Business Research, 1963.

Simon, Paul, "The Illinois Legislature: A Study in Corruption," *Harper's Magazine,* Vol. 229, No. 74, September 1964, pp. 74-5.

Sorauf, Frank J., *Party and Representation: Legislative Politics in Pennsylvania.* New York: Atherton Press, 1963.

Wahlke, John C., Heinz Eulau, William Buchanan, and LeRoy C. Ferguson, *The Legislative System.* New York: John Wiley & Sons, Inc., 1962.

Wheeler, John P., Jr., ed., *Salient Issues of Constitutional Revision.* New York: National Municipal League, 1961.

Zeigler, Harmon, "Interest Groups in the States," in *Politics in the American States,* eds. Herbert Jacob and Kenneth N. Vines. Boston: Little, Brown & Co., 1965, pp. 101-47.

Zeller, Belle, ed., *American State Legislatures.* New York: Thomas Y. Crowell Co., 1954.

Index

A

Abernethy, Byron W., 48
Adams, John, 87-88
Agriculture, 16, 17
  interest groups, 27
  reapportionment and, 82
  state regulatory activities, 13-15
Aid for Families with Dependent Children, 31
Air pollution, 14
Alabama
  characteristics of legislature, 165
  governor's power in, 58
  legislators
    salary, 116
    terms, 130
    turnover, 105
  as a one-party state, 62, 75
  political leadership in, 19
  political parties, 23, 24
  reapportionment, 84
Alaska, 76
  characteristics of legislature, 165
  expenditure patterns, 11, 12
  legislators
    salary, 116
    staff, 145
  political parties, 24
American Farm Bureau Federation, 101
American Legislative Process: Congress and the States (Keefe and Ogul), 106, 143
American Political Science Association, 103, 159
American State Legislatures, 103, 106
American State Legislatures in Mid-Twentieth Century, 159
American State Politics (Key), 22, 109
Anderson, John, 158
Apportionment
  judicial intervention, 73-75
  Supreme Court on, 73-75
Arizona
  characteristics of legislature, 165
  geographic factors, 16
  as a one-party state, 76
  political parties in, 21, 24, 63
  salary of legislators, 116
  taxation, 11
Arkansas
  characteristics of legislature, 165
  expenditure patterns, 12
  governor's power in, 58
  as a one-party state, 62, 75
  political leadership in, 19
  political parties, 23, 24
  salary of legislators, 116

B

Baker v. Carr, 2, 4, 44, 73, 74, 77, 83
Balmer, Donald, 112
Baltimore, political importance of, 33
Barber, James David, 66, 101-2, 110, 124
Bilbo, Theodore, 18
Bill of Rights, 30, 51-52
Buchanan, William, 93, 94, 96, 99, 100
Byrd machine, 19, 21

C

California
  expenditure patterns, 11
  geographic factors, 16
  importance of cities in, 33, 34
  interest groups, 27
  legislators, 100, 101, 114
    campaigning, 112, 113
    election, 109
    salary, 116
  legislature
    behavior of, 55
    characteristics, 165
    leadership, 140
    physical facilities, 135
    reforms, 158